From Churchill's SAS
to Hitler's Waffen-SS

By the same author

Tigers at War:
The Princess of Wales's Royal Regiment
25 Years in Front-Line Modern Conflict
(Helion & Company, 2017)

Special Forces Commander:
The Life and Wars of Peter Wand-Tetley, OBE, MC,
Commando, SAS, SOE and Paratrooper
(Pen & Sword, 2011)

The Royal Rifle Volunteers:
On Operations
(The Royal Rifle Volunteers, 2005)

From Churchill's SAS to Hitler's Waffen-SS

The Secret Wartime Exploits of Captain Douglas Berneville-Claye

by

Michael Scott

Foreword by
Lieutenant General Douglas Chalmers, CB, DSO, OBE

Pen & Sword
MILITARY
AN IMPRINT OF PEN & SWORD BOOKS LTD.
YORKSHIRE – PHILADELPHIA

First published in Great Britain in 2022 by
Pen & Sword Military
An imprint of
Pen & Sword Books Ltd
Yorkshire – Philadelphia

ISBN 978 1 39906 863 5

Printed and bound in the UK by CPI Group (UK) Ltd, Croydon, CR0 4YY.

Pen & Sword Books Limited incorporates the imprints of Atlas, Archaeology, Aviation, Discovery, Family History, Fiction, History, Maritime, Military, Military Classics, Politics, Select, Transport, True Crime, Air World, Frontline Publishing, Leo Cooper, Remember When, Seaforth Publishing, The Praetorian Press, Wharncliffe Local History, Wharncliffe Transport, Wharncliffe True Crime, White Owl and After the Battle.

For a complete list of Pen & Sword titles please contact

PEN & SWORD BOOKS LIMITED
47 Church Street, Barnsley, South Yorkshire, S70 2AS, England
E-mail: enquiries@pen-and-sword.co.uk
Website: www.pen-and-sword.co.uk
or
PEN AND SWORD BOOKS
1950 Lawrence Rd, Havertown, PA 19083, USA
E-mail: Uspen-and-sword@casematepublishers.com
Website: www.penandswordbooks.com

'Of mankind we may say in general they are fickle, hypocritical, and greedy of gain.'

Niccolò Machiavelli

Contents

List of Illustrations

1. Berneville-Claye as a young subaltern, after Sandhurst, having been commissioned into the West Yorkshire Regiment in 1941, with his mother, Daisy Claye. *(Archive / private collection)*
2. Blair 'Paddy' Mayne in 1941, who, in the aftermath of the 1942 Benghazi raid, commanded A Squadron 1st SAS Regiment during Operations LIGHTFOOT and PALMYRA, prior to Berneville-Claye's capture by the enemy in late December 1942. *(IWM MH 24415)*
3. Lieutenant Edward McDonald, as the bearded driver in the foreground of a group of heavily armed jeeps, in one of the most iconic of early SAS wartime images, January 1943. McDonald won the DCM as a sergeant in the Cameron Highlanders, was commissioned from the ranks into the West Yorkshire Regiment, and served in Paddy Mayne's A Squadron, alongside Berneville-Claye. *(IWM E 21337)*
4. Berneville-Claye, with his POW number 35300, photographed at the POW camp, Stammlager (Stalag) VIIIB, at Lamsdorf, Germany, in the autumn of 1943. *(PRO WO 416/28/92)*
5. Portrait sketch of Berneville-Claye, sporting a moustache, while incarcerated as a POW. *(PRO KV 2/626)*
6. Ronald Seth, a British SOE double agent who was infiltrated into the POW camp, Offizierslager (Oflag) 79, at Brunswick, Germany, in October 1944 and maintained that Berneville-Claye was already an informant for the Germans by that stage. *(Archive / private collection)*
7. John Amery, architect of the British Free Corps of the Waffen-SS, with his bigamously married third wife, Michelle Thomas, in a Milan prison courtyard in May 1945, following capture by Italian partisans near Lake Como. He was later executed for high treason. *(IWM NA 24784)*

8. SS-Obergruppenführer (Lieutenant General) Gottlob Berger, Chief of the SS-Hauptamt (Main Office) in Berlin, responsible for SS recruiting and, from July 1944, also the Chief Kriegsgefangenenwesen (Director of POW Camps and Affairs), from whose office in Berlin Berneville-Claye received his Waffen-SS papers. *(Archive / private collection)*

9. SS-Obergruppenführer (Lieutenant General) Felix Steiner, the Waffen-SS corps commander to whom Berneville-Claye reported for duty, and with whom he dined in April 1945, declaring his desire to fight with the Germans against the Russians on the Eastern Front. *(Archive / private collection)*

10. British Free Corps soldiers of the Waffen-SS, Kenneth Berry (left) and Alfred Minchin (right), both wearing the German field-grey uniform, but with an armband on the left cuff, inscribed 'British Free Corps'; a Union Jack badge just above that; and, on the right collar, a black patch with three heraldic lions. *(PRO HO 45/25817 & HO 45/25820)*

11. Thomas Cooper, most sinister of the 'Big Six' of the British Free Corps, present at the formal embodiment of the BFC in January 1944, and prior to that serving with the mainstream Waffen-SS in occupied Poland, and subsequently on the Eastern Front against the Russians. *(Archive / private collection)*

12. 'Our Flag is Going Forward Too' – part of the recruiting literature and series of propaganda posters, designed by John Amery in April 1943 for the nascent 'British Legion of St George', later the 'British Free Corps', before the project was taken out of his hands by the German authorities and passed to the Waffen-SS. *(Archive / private collection)*

13. Eric Pleasants in BFC uniform. Prior to the war, he had made a living as a wrestler, a weightlifter, a circus 'strongman' act, a boxer, and a physical training instructor. While behind bars, for disturbing the peace in Jersey, he met the criminal Eddie Chapman, later to become the British double agent 'Zigzag'. *(Archive / private collection)*

14. William Joyce ('Lord Haw-Haw') on a stretcher (he was shot in the thigh when arrested) being carried into a British 2nd Army hospital,

Acknowledgements

I should like to thank Lieutenant General Douglas Chalmers for writing the foreword to this book. The time that he has taken in his extremely busy schedule to support both this project and previous endeavours, and his wholehearted encouragement, is very much appreciated.

In bringing to fruition an endeavour such as this book, one can't help but be conscious of the metaphor 'standing on the shoulders of giants', and the benefit that one derives from the sheer hard work and scholarship that has preceded one's own efforts. Although the bibliography to this work is comprehensive, one feels obliged to highlight a few particularly noteworthy authors in this regard. The wartime memoirs of Malcolm James Pleydell, Carol Mather, Fitzroy Maclean and Geoffrey Gordon-Creed did much to put flesh on the bones of the official SAS reports.

Ronald Seth and Adrian Weale have done more than anyone to develop our understanding of the British Free Corps and place its activities in context. The personal courage and painstaking research of Margaret Metcalfe into her family history did much to illuminate her natural father's personal life. It is also sometimes the case that a single article can highlight an avenue for an important new line of enquiry, and in this instance one such article by Stephen Holt did just that.

Thanks must go to libraries and their staff in both England and Australia. Special mention must be made of the Imperial War Museum and the UK National Archives, and their staff, and the excellent facilities provided in terms of making available official documentation. Particularly in this regard, declassified British Security Service (MI5) intelligence files.

My gratitude also goes to David Pannell and Linne Matthews, who have spent numerous hours checking the typescript. I should like to thank them for their considerable care and patience, for the book is undoubtedly a great deal better for their suggestions, corrections, and advice. Nonetheless, any mistakes made, which given the sweep of history is a distinct possibility, are entirely mine. Finally, I would like to express my thanks to my wife, Deborah, for her assistance with the maps and her unfailing support throughout this venture.

Foreword

By Lieutenant General Douglas Chalmers,
CB, DSO, OBE

The last prosecutions for treason in the United Kingdom occurred in the aftermath of the Second World War. Two civilian traitors, John Amery and William Joyce ('Lord Haw-Haw'), both propagandists working for the Nazis, were found guilty and hanged. Two other men, Thomas Cooper, of the Waffen-SS, and Walter Purdy, a merchant seaman, were found guilty of treason but had their sentences commuted to life imprisonment.

Five British subjects were prosecuted under the Treachery Act of 1940. Duncan Scott-Ford, a merchant seaman, and Theodore Schurch, a Royal Army Service Corps soldier, were prosecuted, found guilty and hanged for their treachery. Three civilians, George Armstrong, Oswald Job and Jose Key, a Gibraltarian saboteur, were also tried, found guilty, and hanged. Dorothy O'Grady, from the Isle of Wight, was found guilty of treachery, but her death sentence was commuted to imprisonment.

Two other treacherous malefactors who, no doubt, would have been sentenced to death, met their demise before official execution. Harold Cole, a Royal Engineers soldier, betrayed many in the French Resistance but, following his escape from custody, was shot dead in a gunfight with the French Police. New Zealand-born Patrick Heenan, of the British Indian Army, was found guilty of espionage by court martial but, it would seem, was shot dead by a guard before he had formally been sentenced.

In the aftermath of the war, just shy of 200 British suspects, including Captain Douglas Berneville-Claye, were investigated as 'renegades or persons suspected of assisting the enemy'. Of these, some 140 were prosecuted, generally not specifically for treason, but under the auspices of the Treachery Act of 1940 or by courts martial, for lesser charges. This number included some thirty-nine renegades who at some stage had joined the British Free Corps of the Waffen-SS, and fifteen who had worked as Nazi radio propagandists.

Committing treason or treachery breaks a very powerful and deep-rooted social and cultural taboo. Expectations placed on British Army officers, in terms of leadership, integrity, and moral and physical courage, are extremely high, as indeed should be the case for those placed in a unique position of authority and responsibility. Investigated by the British Security Service for collaborating with the enemy while he was a prisoner of war and for his association with the British Free Corps, Berneville-Claye's story – both while serving in the British Army and as a civilian – is an extraordinary one.

Full of dishonesty, deceit and betrayal, one fears there are aspects of Berneville-Claye's life that will never be satisfactorily clarified. However, the author's comprehensive and skilful research has done a fine job of establishing the facts underpinning the tale of one of Britain's most infamous and inglorious men to emerge from the Second World War.

In telling this incredible and at times bewildering story, the author breathes life into the tale of this complex, deceitful, yet profoundly fascinating man. Yet the book also has other merits besides. In applying his analytical skills, the author has examined the myriad layers of exaggeration, secrecy and obfuscation surrounding this case. This is important, for historians always seek corroborating documentary evidence, and in Berneville-Claye's case it is essential.

The narrative is also particularly merit-worthy for a further reason. Although vigorously pursuing the truth, the author examines Berneville-Claye's life without prejudice, conscious that although flawed, it is nonetheless worthy of serious and objective assessment.

This is a tough historical subject area with which to get to grips, and this book is an authoritative and worthy effort. It is an insightful read.

Master of Emmanuel College, Cambridge
Colonel Commandant, The Queen's Division of Infantry

Introduction

Most families, if they search carefully and far enough into their genealogy, are likely to find a black sheep of the family. In 2002, Margaret Metcalfe published *All My Father's Children*, which chronicled her personal odyssey, over the preceding two years, to discover her natural father, Douglas Berneville-Claye, and through him her wider family.

What Metcalfe discovered was shocking, for her research uncovered deeply uncomfortable truths and uncertainties. Her quest also brought her joy and sadness in equal measure. For there were those of her newly discovered family who were delighted she had found them. But also, those who, on account of her revelations, would rather she had let sleeping dogs lie, and for whom she became a target of their opprobrium.

However, Berneville-Claye's details were already in the public domain. Ronald Seth's book, *Jackals of The Reich*, published in 1972, used pseudonyms, but it is not overly difficult to identify, in Chapter 15, the real 'Archibald Webster'. Then, in 1994, Adrian Weale published *Renegades* (revised in 2002), in which all names he used were real. These days, of course, the Internet also has a significant part to play, and Berneville-Claye is honoured with his own Wikipedia entry.

Berneville-Claye courted controversy and infamy throughout his life. A precocious youth, he developed into a handsome and charismatic young man, although his moral compass was very often disinclined to point true. Given his natural talents and charm, no doubt he could have made a very genuine success of himself in the conventional sense, but instead he consistently chose to take short cuts, frequently on the wrong side of the law. In and out of court and prison throughout his life, he was court-martialled and cashiered from the British Army, was a confidence trickster, a villain, a serial philanderer, twice a bigamist, the father of some ten children (the majority born out of wedlock), a consistent liar and fantasist.

However, it is Berneville-Claye's Second World War exploits that remain arguably the most intriguing and enigmatic, and which are the primary focus of this narrative. Commissioned as an officer at the Royal Military Academy, Sandhurst, he later wore the uniforms of both the British SAS and Nazi SS. As a prisoner of war, incarcerated in wartime Germany, his fellow inmates and the British Security Service, MI5, were convinced of his treachery. Seemingly a stool pigeon, German informant, and a renegade officer of the British Free Corps – the Waffen-SS unit composed of British and Commonwealth subjects – the true nature and full extent of his alleged wartime treachery remains, however, elusive.

This is Berneville-Claye's extraordinary and fantastical story.

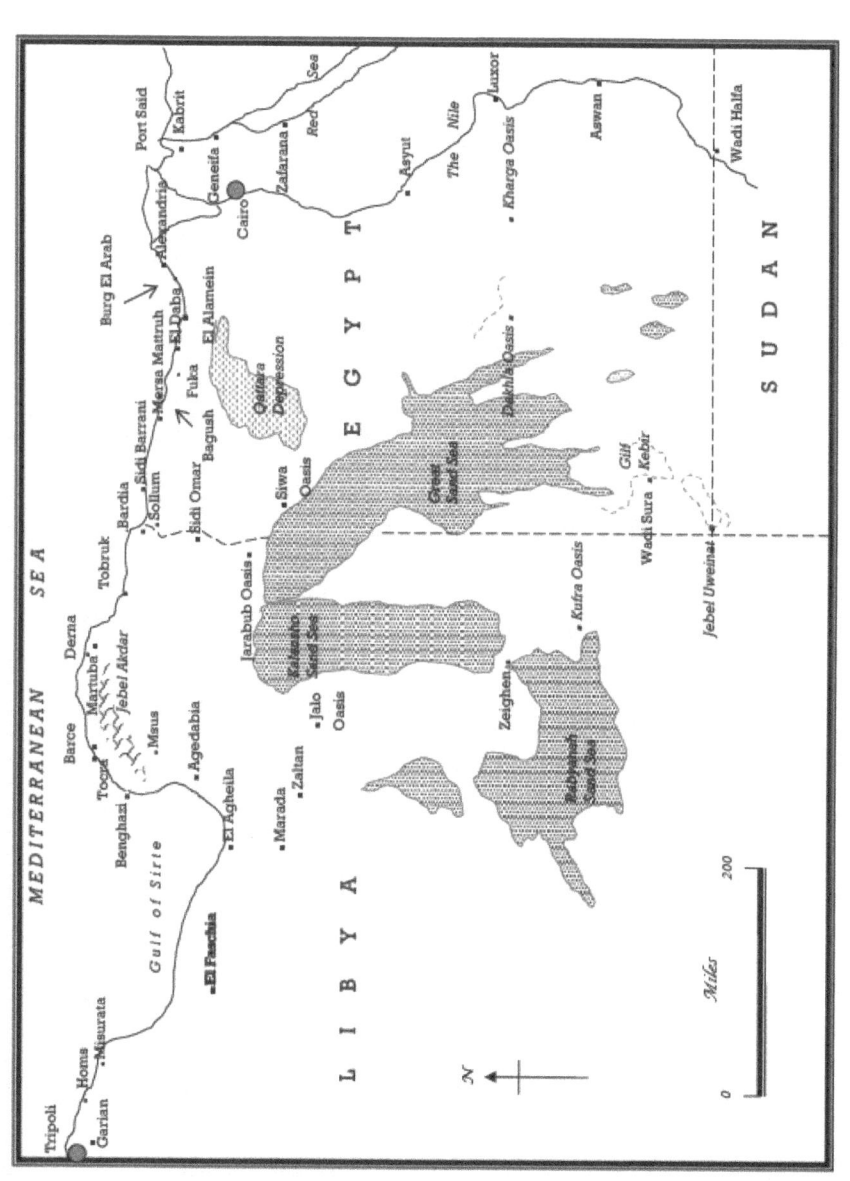

Map 1. Northeast Africa.

Map 2. Germany.

Chapter 1

Early Life and Military Training

Douglas Berneville Webster Claye came into this world on 26 November 1917, near Woolwich, London. He was born at his parents' home, 143 Sandy Hill Road, in the hilly suburb of Plumstead. The following month, on 23 December, he was baptised in the Parish Church of St Margaret, Plumstead, within the Royal Borough of Greenwich.[1] His subsequent self-aggrandisement of his name to the smart-sounding, double-barrelled Douglas Webster St Aubyn Berneville-Claye, achieved by adding one of his given names to make the hyphenated 'Berneville-Claye', occurred much later. But where 'St Aubyn' came from is unknown. Never to do things by halves, as we shall see, he also later provided himself with a fictitious aristocratic title, 'Lord Charlesworth'. Although he did not adopt his hyphenated name until later, to avoid confusion we will hereafter refer to him as Berneville-Claye.

His father, Frederick ('Fred') Wainwright Claye, and his mother, Daisy (née Jackson), were married in Woolwich Register Office on 14 September 1912. At some stage prior to his marriage, Fred added an 'e' to his original surname, Clay, to become Claye. Fred was 29 when he married, and their marriage certificate records that he was, at the time, a sergeant in the Army Service Corps. The ASC was founded in December 1888. Later, following the First World War, the corps gained the 'Royal' prefix to become the RASC. It has since become the Royal Logistic Corps (RLC), the largest corps in the British Army.

Douglas's mother, Daisy, sometimes referred to as Decima, was 21 when she married. Their marriage certificate does not record an occupation for her, but gives her father's name as Henry Philip Jackson, solicitor's clerk, deceased. Later in life she is recorded as

Daisy Claye on her husband's death certificate, and as Decima Claye on her son's discharge from the 12th Lancers. However, her name is recorded as Kettle-Jackson on her son's POW record card, and as Decima Kettle-Webster on his death certificate. It may seem that Berneville-Claye was not the only one in his family to play fast and loose with their name.

During the 1881 census, Fred Claye's father, Charles Henry Clay, was recorded as age 23, a glass-bottle blower in Hunslet, Leeds. He later married Fanny (née Webster), of Beeston, Leeds, from a family of labourers. At the time of the census Fred's grandfather, Charley Clay, was recorded as age 51, and listed as a 'stuff finisher', working in the textile industry. This is evidently all solid, working–class parentage, from the industrial north. Thus, Berneville-Claye's later pretensions to aristocratic parentage were pure invention.

At the time of his birth, Berneville-Claye's father, Fred, was serving with the Army in Woolwich. Berneville-Claye had an elder brother, Derek Claye, born in 1914, and a sister, Kate. Derek Claye had a son, Brian Claye, born in 1942, who later married Lorraine, and together they had three children. Fred and Daisy Claye also brought up as their own son a nephew, Rupert Clay (without an 'e'), born in 1921, the illegitimate son of one of Fred's two sisters. Rupert later tragically died in a road accident, in 1955, as a private soldier serving in the West Yorkshire Regiment.

Fred Claye had a long and successful career in the Army, rising through the ranks, commencing as a private soldier in the Boer War and retiring in the rank of captain in 1920. In the 1919 King's Birthday Honours List he was awarded the MBE (military division), as a staff quartermaster sergeant, for service in the First World War. Specifically, for 'valuable service rendered in connection with military operations in France'. From December 1933 until November 1936, Fred and Daisy became public house licensees of the Green Tree Inn, Little Ouseburn, deep in the Yorkshire countryside. Fred died of cancer in 1965, aged 83, and Daisy is shown as his widow on his death certificate, although she had earlier left him.

On 4 March 1933, Berneville-Claye enlisted as a boy soldier at Sheffield and joined the Army Technical School (ATS) at Chepstow. Ordinarily three years in length, the course prepared a soldier for the military technical trades and as a non-commissioned officer (NCO). 'Boy service' was reckoned as from 15 to 18 years of age. Thereafter one was expected to serve eight years with the colours, i.e. with the Regular Army, and then for a further four years with the Reserve. While serving on the Reserve one was liable to be called back to the colours in the event of an emergency or war.

However, on 13 August 1934, Berneville-Claye was discharged from the ATS, Chepstow, having completed just eighteen months of the three-year course, as 'services no longer required' – a term that falls short of any suggestion of misconduct. His conduct was listed as 'very good', so he may just not have had the right aptitude, or attitude. It may be that he had only joined at the behest of his father (a career soldier) and perhaps his heart was not in it. His discharge address is given as the Green Tree Inn, Little Ouseburn, thus he evidently returned home to his parents after leaving Chepstow.

In the late summer of 1934, Berneville-Claye, aged 16 and having recently been discharged from the ATS, met Ada Mary Metcalfe. She was 22 at the time; born in 1911, she was to die in 1975 of asthma and heart disease. Ada was working as a scullery maid at the Green Tree Inn, which Fred and Daisy Claye were running. Ada lived just across from the inn, in a row of small cottages. The young Berneville-Claye and Ada had a relatively short-lived affair, perhaps of some three months, but with significant consequences.

At the end of that year, on 5 December 1934, shortly after having got Ada Metcalfe pregnant, Berneville-Claye joined 16th/5th Queen's Royal Lancers at York. (Following amalgamation with 17th/21st Lancers in 1993, the regiment became the Queen's Royal Lancers.) Ada wrote to both Berneville-Claye and his commanding officer concerning her condition, but to no avail. His commanding officer responded to her by letter, in which he stated, 'Boy Claye is unlikely to proceed abroad in the near future.' From this, one might surmise that she had stressed that she had not heard from him and had thus asked whether he had been posted away or abroad. The letter she received back from Berneville-Claye denied any involvement in her pregnancy and warned her that if she persisted in this vein, he would refute any such allegation in every possible way.[2]

In due course, on 10 August 1935, Ada gave birth to a daughter, Margaret ('Maggie') Metcalfe, out of wedlock. Maggie was the first of some ten children that Berneville-Claye eventually sired. In time, Maggie became a midwife and, with her first husband, Brian Underhill, whom she married in 1957, she had two daughters, Helen, born in 1961 in Cyprus, and Liz, born in 1963. Helen and her husband Frank subsequently provided Maggie with three grandchildren: Francesca, Daniel and Genevieve. Following Brian's death in 1992, Maggie became a widow, but subsequently met, in 1997, Barry Stoll, and married him in 2002.

Berneville-Claye served as a boy soldier with 16th/5th Queen's Royal Lancers until his eighteenth birthday on 26 November 1935. He then served on as a private soldier (or, in cavalry parlance, trooper) until he was discharged on 19 June 1936, for the second time in his young life as 'services no longer required'. Nonetheless, during those eighteen months with the regiment, while based in York, he received excellent tuition on riding and the general care of horses. This stood him in very good stead a little later in terms of gaining employment.

In the summer of 1936, having left the Army, Berneville-Claye travelled down to Surrey, where he duly secured a job as a riding instructor at the local stables. He lodged in a room over the stables and while working there he met Irene May Palmer. Within a couple of months they married, legitimately, on 4 October 1936, in the Parish Church of St Nicholas, Thames Ditton. Their marriage certificate gives his age as 20, although he was in fact just a month shy of 19. His occupation is given as 'riding instructor', and that of his father as 'Retired Army Officer'; both are true, for his father was an Army captain upon his retirement. Irene's father, Charles Palmer, is recorded as deceased, and she gives her home as 5 Bridge Cottages, Thames Ditton.

However, the following year, Berneville-Claye left his first wife, Irene, while she was pregnant with their daughter, Yvonne, who was subsequently born on 23 June 1937. Having disappeared without telling her, Irene next heard of Berneville-Claye a decade later, in a tabloid newspaper, *News of the World*, following his April 1946 court martial. Moreover, Yvonne never heard from or saw her father in all the years that she was growing up. Her mother later met a new partner, with whom she had two sons. However, it was some time before her mother felt Yvonne was old enough to be told that these were her half-brothers and that the man whom she had assumed was her father was in fact her step-father.

Berneville-Claye rejoined the Army on 24 August 1937. This time he enlisted with 12th (Prince of Wales's) Royal Lancers. He joined up at Barrow-in-Furness, Cumbria, and provided a home address in Leeds. (Following amalgamation with 9th Queen's Royal Lancers in 1960, the regiment became 9th/12th Royal Lancers (Prince of Wales's); and after a subsequent amalgamation in 2015 with the Queen's Royal Lancers, it became the Royal Lancers (Queen Elizabeth's Own).)

The 12th Royal Lancers had arrived back in England, from Egypt, in November 1936. During most of 1937 they were based in Tidworth, before moving to Aldershot in 1938. During Berneville-Claye's initial period of service, he achieved the 3rd and 2nd Class Army Certificates of Education, on 6 and 10 October 1937 respectively. However, some thirteen months after having joined, he was discharged from the Army, on 5 October 1938, for the third time as 'services no longer required'. He provided his discharge address as being in Twickenham, not so far from Thames Ditton, where he had married and subsequently deserted his first wife, Irene. However, during this period of service with the 12th Royal Lancers he never declared to the Army that he was married.

A pattern was thus starting to emerge, for it seems Berneville-Claye was unable to hold down employment as a soldier in the Army for any significant period. One can only surmise why this might have been the case. Did he lack the necessary self-discipline and organisation; or perhaps he lacked the necessary stamina, determination and work ethic? Maybe he was not enough of a team player, or perhaps he was found to be overly troublesome to his peers and superiors? Perhaps it was a combination of a number or all of these factors.

Following his Army discharge, from 5 October 1938 until the summer of 1939 it seems possible that Berneville-Claye may have worked as a freelance journalist in London and then later in Leeds, although there is limited evidence of this. Regardless, in June 1939 Berneville-Claye met a girl, Nina Kathleen Payne, in Torquay, on England's southern coastline, and saved her from potential drowning in the sea. He informed Nina that he was single, and the following year she became his second wife, albeit bigamously.

One may assume that Nina was heavily pregnant by the time they married, for the *News of the World*, when later reporting upon disclosures at Berneville-Claye's first bigamy trial, on 30 June 1946, states that 'owing to her condition they went through a ceremony of marriage' some nine months after first meeting. Moreover, regarding his occupation, when Nina first met him, she stated that she was under the impression he was working as a journalist in Leeds. This appears to corroborate his job as that of a freelance journalist. It also seems that prior to their marriage he may have lodged, at some stage in 1939, with the Payne family in Horsforth, about 5 miles from Leeds.

The Second World War commenced on 1 September 1939 with Germany's invasion of Poland, and on 3 September, Britain declared war on Germany. Berneville-Claye signed up and joined the Royal Air Force within a week, on 8 September, as an RAF aircrew trainee at Cardington. From here he went to Cambridge for aircrew training. This was the fourth period of military service within six years that he had embarked upon. His first ten weeks were spent at an Initial Training Wing. Thereafter he attended an Elementary Flying Training School for five to six months, a role that Marshall's of Cambridge (now Marshall Aerospace), amongst other firms, provided at the time.

as aircrew training in the 1930s and early 1940s was carried out not only by the RAF, but also by several civilian firms.

Marshall Aerospace, based at Cambridge, fulfilled the role of Number 22 Flying Training School in the late 1930s and early 1940s. Trainees were accommodated in the Airport Hotel or in private lodgings around Cambridge, as well as some in the North Court at Emmanuel College. It is probable that this experience provided Berneville-Claye with the basis and inspiration to later fabricate that he had graduated from Emmanuel College, Cambridge University. However, on 27 March 1940, Berneville-Claye was discharged from the RAF as 'unlikely to make an efficient pilot', this now being his fourth such discharge from the military.

After the war, at Berneville-Claye's June 1946 bigamy trial, Nina is reported as saying in court that the reason for Berneville-Claye's RAF dismissal was that he had failed a mathematics exam. Ronald Seth, in his book on the British Free Corps, suggests the reason was because he had gone absent without leave (AWOL) to marry the heavily pregnant Nina. His dismissal may well have been for a combination of both these reasons.

Berneville-Claye's discharge, after several months and thus close to the end of his training, was just three days after he had married Nina on 24 March 1940. This, Berneville-Claye's second marriage, was to be his first bigamous marriage, for he was still married to Irene, with whom he had a daughter, Yvonne, both of whom he had abandoned in 1937. His new bride, Nina, was 24. They married at Otley Register Office, near Leeds. He gives his age on the marriage certificate as 26, although in fact he was 22, and his occupation as 'cadet pilot RAF, former journalist'. He gives his father's occupation as 'Lieutenant General HM Forces'. This was a significant embellishment upon fact since his father had reached the relatively junior rank of captain in the RASC and thereafter, from December 1933 to November 1936, had become a public house licensee.

Shortly after they were married, Berneville-Claye and Nina rented a white cottage in Great Ouseburn, close to the village of Little Ouseburn where he had abandoned Ada Metcalfe and their daughter, Maggie. From Berneville-Claye's marriage with Nina there was a son, Graeme, who when young went to the local school in Great Ouseburn, the same school that Maggie Metcalfe, albeit some five years his senior, was also still attending.

Of course, at the time neither Graeme nor Maggie knew that they were half-siblings. However, apparently it was common knowledge, amongst the adults of the two villages and the local vicinity, that Berneville-Claye was also Maggie's father, and this could not have always been comfortable for their family and acquaintances. Berneville-Claye's second and thus his first bigamous marriage, to Nina, only came to light many years later, after the war, at Berneville-Claye's court martial in April 1946.

In due course, Graeme became a captain in the Merchant Navy, and married Gloria. In fact, having left private school in Leeds at the age of 16, Graeme went to sea, and his first voyage as a deck officer cadet was over two years long. Years later, Graeme and Gloria both became authors. In his autobiography Graeme mentions little about his father, other than to confirm that he had very little to do with his upbringing or education. Gloria's debut novel concerns the story of two army officers and their post-war wealth creation schemes and foray into smuggling. The English officer, a certain Captain Douglas Coulter, is clearly inspired by Berneville-Claye, with other parallels also in play. The names of a few other characters in the novel, such as Irene and Nina, are also echoes of those from real life.

Following Berneville-Claye's discharge from the RAF in March 1940, it is believed he took up employment in an aircraft factory in Leeds. On 2 December that same year, he joined the Leeds Home Guard. He was arrested a little later that month for posing as an RAF officer. This came to light when he was involved in a car crash, sporting RAF pilot's wings on his uniform, for while subsequently at the officers' convalescent home, he stole some cheques. This resulted in him being tried, on 5 January 1941, at the Magistrates Court, Leeds West Riding Quarter Sessions, for impersonating an officer and for theft of cheques – specifically: stealing cheques, forging cheques, uttering forged cheques, and two cases of false pretences. However, by paying back the stolen money, he was sentenced only to be fined and bound over for two years.[3]

It was around this stage, in January 1941, that he started referring to himself by his invented moniker, the Honourable Douglas St Aubyn Webster Berneville-Claye. Moreover, he evidently also cultivated a 'smart' accent, to complement the aristocratic family background he had invented for himself. His accent was later described as British 'old-school-tie', 'educated' and 'cultured'. He next enlisted in the West Yorkshire Regiment and, on 16 January 1941, was posted as a private soldier to the Infantry Training Centre (ITC) of the West Yorkshire Regiment. This was therefore the fifth period of military training that he had embarked upon.

Nonetheless, he did not stay in the ranks overly long. He falsely claimed to have been educated at Charterhouse (a prestigious independent boarding school in Godalming, Surrey), and subsequently at Magdalen College, Oxford and Emmanuel College, Cambridge. These details were noted on his Army Service Record.

As a result of fabricating this seemingly impressive academic background, Berneville-Claye was selected for officer training. But whether, more importantly, he possessed 'effective intelligence' or the *sine qua non* for an Army officer, leadership ability, was to be tested in the months ahead. He duly attended the Royal Military Academy, Sandhurst, on a short war course, for an 'Emergency Commission'. This was his sixth course of military training within several years. His Sandhurst entry records him as 'Douglas Webster St Aubyn Berneville-Claye', with a college entry date of 6 June 1941, a departure date of 26 September 1941, and as being commissioned into the West Yorkshire Regiment.[4]

Given Berneville-Claye's disposition for failing to complete military training courses, somewhat surprisingly this time, he prevailed. No doubt the relatively brief nature of the Sandhurst short war course and associated Emergency Commission was a factor, never, in his case, testing him over a sustained enough period to identify leadership flaws, which later came to light. Regardless, he successfully passed out of Sandhurst with a Grade C (on a scale of A, B, C, D, all of which were pass grades). Moreover, he did so without any adverse comments on his report and served the same amount of training time at Sandhurst as all other cadets. He was gazetted on 10 October 1941, with an Emergency Commission, in the rank of second lieutenant, and an Army Number of 207721.[5] He was one of five subalterns from his intake who joined the West Yorkshire Regiment, and he was posted to the 11th Battalion of the regiment.

During the Second World War, a dozen battalions of the West Yorkshire Regiment were raised. The 1st and 2nd battalions were both Regular; the former served throughout the war in South-East Asia and Burma, the latter, first in the Middle East and subsequently in South-East Asia and Burma. The remainder, including the 11th Battalion, to which Berneville-Claye was posted, were Territorial Army units, generally with a role in Home Forces and to reinforce the two overseas Regular battalions.

In October 1941, when Berneville-Claye was posted to 11th West Yorkshires, it was part of 203rd Infantry Brigade of the Devon & Cornwall Division, and was stationed at Albany Barracks, Parkhurst on the Isle of Wight, under command of Lieutenant Colonel W.H. Green, MC.[6] Berneville-Claye reported for duty on 6 October, with several other subalterns, and was posted to B Company. Here he quickly found himself involved with the rest of his unit in building anti-tank defences during the day. These resembled long scaffolding poles, some 18 feet in length, buried 3 feet into the ground and sloping towards the direction of the sea, like a giant pike. At night the battalion conducted anti-invasion patrols of the coastline, in readiness for any enemy incursion.

In late November 1941, the 11th West Yorkshires moved from the Isle of Wight to temporary accommodation at Sturminster Newton, Dorset. There, on 4 December, the battalion was visited by their new brigade commander, Brigadier J.G. Frere, DSO, MC. By the end of the first week of December, the battalion was on the move again, this time to its new permanent accommodation in Yeovil, Somerset. It evidently kept itself busy training reinforcements for its two Regular battalions, for later that same month, 100 other ranks were selected from the battalion to form a draft for overseas service.

Early in the new year, on 2 January 1942, Berneville-Claye was transferred from B Company to C Company, in what appears to have been a routine move within the battalion. Shortly thereafter he was also selected, with one other subaltern from the battalion, to attend a four-week course, from 11 January to 6 February, at 5 Corps Junior Leaders Wing.

However, having managed to keep his nose clean during officer training at Sandhurst, within three months of having been commissioned, Berneville-Claye was placed under close arrest, on 13 January 1942, pending trial by court martial.[7] This was on account of presenting worthless cheques on several different occasions. As a result, on 6 March 1942 he attended trial at Sherborne, Dorset. This was the first of three courts martial at which he would stand trial during his Army career, the subsequent two occasions being after the war, in 1946.

At this first court martial, at Sherborne Castle, he was found guilty on seven charges under Section 40 of the Army Act, in respect of dishonoured cheques, although it seems that the associated Section 16 charges were dropped. There is a copy of a report to this effect from Berneville-Claye's War Office personal file, dated 12 May 1942, signed by Colonel R.E. Barnwell of the Adjutant General's department.

In the interim, during February 1942, the 11th West Yorkshires moved once again, this time north to Bridlington, in the East Riding of Yorkshire. But the battalion was not destined to remain in Yorkshire for long and was subsequently posted overseas, in mid-June 1942, to the Falkland Islands.[8] However, Berneville-Claye remained behind in Dorset to attend his court martial. During this period, for the purposes of accommodation, he was temporarily attached to the 5th Battalion, King's Shropshire Light Infantry, based in Sherborne, as recorded in Barnwell's report.

Barnwell's report states: 'He [Berneville-Claye] is 24 years of age and was granted an Emergency Commission from an O.C.T.U. [Officer Cadet Training Unit] on 27.09.1941. He was educated at Charterhouse, Oxford and Cambridge and is a Barrister in civil life.' The report goes on to record: 'The accused conducted his own defence with a good deal of skill and was able to satisfy the court that, with respect to the Section 16 charges, the cause of the cheques being dishonoured was neglect on his part rather than dishonesty.' Accordingly, Berneville-Claye was sentenced only to be reprimanded, with the court martial proceedings later confirmed, on 23 March, by the General Officer Commanding (GOC)-in Chief, Southern Command.[9]

It is noteworthy that Berneville-Claye conducted his own defence, successfully passing himself off, to the prosecution and his Army superiors presiding at his court martial, as a barrister in civilian life. This he managed, even though his Army Service Record listed his pre-war career as a journalist, with no suggestion that he had ever studied law. Moreover, he appears to have been both convincing and successful in the role, thus demonstrating an early talent as a confidence trickster. In later life he also enjoyed amateur dramatics, and this suggests a precocious and convincing talent in this regard.

There is no disputing the fact that Berneville-Claye was extremely talented. The tragedy was that he continued to consistently misuse his talents throughout his life. Those who knew him declared that as a young man he had film-star looks, resembling a young Errol Flynn, that he could 'charm the birds out of the trees', and that few women could resist him. He was 5 feet 7 or 8 inches tall, broad, and muscular for his height, some 150 pounds in weight, with blue-grey eyes and fair hair. He was evidently a handsome, precocious young man, self-confident and assured. Men also tended to find him charismatic, persuasive and convincing.

Nonetheless, it appears that his commanding officer took a very dim view of events surrounding the court martial. Berneville-Claye's Army Service Record confirms that by the following month, 23 April

1942, he was posted out of 11th Battalion, West Yorkshire Regiment, to the 2/5th Battalion, West Yorkshire Regiment. One may reasonably surmise the reason for this was that if any of the dishonoured cheques had been presented to fellow officers within the 11th Battalion, then his position within the officers' mess was untenable. Moreover, a posting on attachment to another unit provided him with the opportunity for a relatively fresh start following his court martial.

Based in Folkestone, under command of Lieutenant Colonel V.M.V. Tighe, the 2/5th West Yorkshires had recently moved there, in mid-March, from Lydd. Then, on 13 June, the 2/5th Battalion's war diary records that Berneville-Claye was 'struck off strength on embarkation overseas'.[10] For its part, the 2/5th West Yorkshires, a Home Defence battalion, converted later that year to the armour role, becoming the 113th Regiment Royal Armoured Corps. However, the soldiers continued to wear their West Yorkshire cap badge on the black beret of the RAC.

Thus, Berneville-Claye's sojourn in Kent with 2/5th West Yorkshires was extremely short-lived. According to his Army Service Record, by 22 June he had been assigned and posted to the Infantry Base Depot, Geneifa, in Egypt. One might surmise that initially this may have been with a view to him joining the 2nd Battalion, West Yorkshire Regiment, which at that time was based in Tobruk, Libya, as part of 9th Indian Brigade of the 5th Indian Division, part of Eighth Army, serving under British Forces Middle East.

The troopship in which Berneville-Claye sailed to Egypt travelled via the Cape of Good Hope, because the Mediterranean route, although shorter in distance, was considered significantly more dangerous to enemy attack. Having departed England's shores, in all likelihood from Liverpool, the ship first headed west with its convoy out into the Atlantic, endeavouring to avoid enemy submarines lurking offshore. If attacked by enemy torpedoes, the convoy's escort of destroyers, corvettes or cruisers engaged their opponents by dropping numerous depth charges into the water. Meanwhile, the vulnerable troopships would make full speed out of the danger zone.

Sweeping around in a large arc, the convoy then headed south and, likely, first anchored briefly at Freetown, Sierra Leone, to take on board fuel and water for the voyage ahead. Having left Freetown, the ship continued steaming south, and a day later crossed the equator. At this stage, no doubt the ship's commanding officer invited Neptune to come aboard to oversee the Crossing the Line ceremony. For those to be initiated, this was ordinarily a lively and raucous affair that seldom few involved forgot.

Thereafter, having reached Cape Town, the ship spent a couple of days berthed alongside the quay. While there, Berneville-Claye and the other troops conducted early morning route marches for exercise, pleased to have firm ground once again under their feet, and were then granted shore leave from noon until midnight. The Cape Town citizens were renowned during the war for their generous hospitality and desire to ensure that visiting troops enjoyed their brief sojourn in their pleasant city.

Having sailed from Cape Town, and perhaps having stopped once more at Durban, the ship continued steaming up the east coast of Africa, past the towns of Dar es Salaam, Tanga and Mombasa. She then entered the Gulf of Aden, cruised up the Red Sea and finally dropped anchor at Suez. Such a trip from England to Egypt generally took six to eight weeks. If the weather was pleasant, then so generally was the trip. But if not, then for those who did not quickly gain their sea legs, elements of the voyage could prove to be something of an ordeal.

Having disembarked at Port Suez, those in the infantry, such as Berneville-Claye, were invariably first dispatched to the Infantry Base Depot, Geneifa. Here they were issued with their full complement of tropical uniform and equipment if they had not already received it on board ship. They then had several weeks to train and acclimatise in the harsh conditions, before joining their regiments in theatre.

Thus, when Berneville-Claye set sail for North Africa, at the age of 24, he already had his first court martial under his belt, after just four months of commissioned service as an officer. Moreover, he left in his wake an illegitimate daughter, Maggie, with Ada Metcalfe, whom he had disowned; a second daughter, Yvonne, from his first wife, Irene (née Palmer), whom he had abandoned; and a son, Graeme, from his second wife Nina (née Payne), whom he had bigamously married.

Chapter 2

L Detachment SAS – Operation BIGAMY

Berneville-Claye arrived in Egypt at a turning point in the Desert War. Whether there had ever been a tentative plan for him to join 2nd Battalion, West Yorkshire Regiment, based at Tobruk remains unclear. Regardless, any such plan never came to fruition, not least because Tobruk fell to enemy forces in June 1942, the same month Berneville-Claye arrived in North Africa. Moreover, while still training and acclimatising at the Infantry Base Depot, Geneifa, it is evident that he volunteered to join L Detachment Special Air Service, during a trawl as his Army Service Record states that he joined the SAS on 20 August 1942. Upon joining the SAS Berneville-Claye almost immediately took part in the ill-fated Benghazi raid, dubbed by the military planners Operation BIGAMY. However, before considering BIGAMY in any detail, first it is worth briefly examining the military context within which this raid took place.

Stalemate had existed between Allied and Axis forces in North Africa since February 1942. Then, in mid-June, the entire British Eighth Army, under Lieutenant General Neil Ritchie, started to withdraw in the face of Rommel's Panzerarmee Afrika. Forced back from the Gazala–Bir Hakeim line, just west of Tobruk, the Eighth Army subsequently started to dig in on the El Alamein line, where it eventually managed to halt the enemy's advance. However, Tobruk and its garrison of the 2nd New Zealand Division fell to Rommel, who took some 33,000 Allied prisoners. Hitler promoted Rommel, the 'Desert Fox', to field marshal (at just 50, the youngest in the Heer) and with this success came an international reputation. Within several days, General Sir Claude Auchinleck had dismissed Ritchie and assumed field command of Eighth Army himself in addition to his role as C–in–C Middle East.

The Desert War had been a campaign in which Axis forces and the Allies had, in turn, pursued one another back and forth across the Libyan Desert. In this fast-paced campaign, the success or failure of operations was often dependent upon logistical capability. The further a force advanced from its secure bases, then it and its lines of communication became increasingly stretched and vulnerable. From Alexandria, held by the British in the east, to Rommel's main supply harbour of Tripoli in the west, was some 1,400 miles; a veritable 'tactician's paradise, but quartermaster's hell'. Nicknamed the 'Benghazi stakes', the aim was to outmanoeuvre one's enemy, whether by withdrawing to a new defensive line, or by advancing and endeavouring to break through and inflict destruction upon his rear echelons.

With Rommel and his Panzerarmee Afrika now facing the Allies at El Alamein, some 50 miles from Alexandria and 150 from Cairo, GHQ Middle East issued the order to start burning its classified documents on 1 July, 'Ash Wednesday', otherwise known as 'The Flap'. Then, deploying all its available troops to the defence of Cairo and the Delta, GHQ prepared for the worst. If the Nile Delta fell into Rommel's hands, so too would the Suez Canal, and beyond the Sinai Desert and Palestine lay the key oilfields of Persia.

Fortunately, El Alamein was tactically excellent for defence. At just 40 miles in length, the line was relatively short, with its northern end on the coastal salt lakes, while its southern end was based upon the quicksand of the Qattara Depression. Hitherto, Axis forces had managed to turn every other Allied defensive line, because the southern ends of such lines invariably lay in open desert. However, stalemate ensued again in July, for Rommel was successful in containing every one of the Eighth Army's counteroffensives against his forces.

Nonetheless, significant changes were afoot. In early August, Churchill flew to Cairo and, disappointed with the lack of success on the El Alamein line, removed Auchinleck from command and appointed General Sir Harold Alexander as the new C-in-C Middle East. Initially, Ritchie's successor was to have been Lieutenant General William 'Strafer' Gott, who had previously commanded 7th Armoured Division (The Desert Rats) and XIII Corps. However, while flying out to Egypt, Gott was killed when his plane was shot down, and Bernard Montgomery was selected as his replacement.

Thus, Montgomery flew out from England to assume command of the experienced Eighth Army, comprising the British 1st, 7th and 10th Armoured divisions, the 44th, 50th and 51st Infantry divisions, and Commonwealth infantry divisions from South Africa, Australia, New Zealand and India. Generals Alexander and Montgomery both reiterated Auchinleck's earlier stance, that Allied forces would stand firm and withdraw no further east than the El Alamein line. In this endeavour they secured early success, by repulsing Rommel's attack on 30 August, in the Battle of Alam el Halfa.

By this stage, GHQ Middle East had ordered Major David Stirling, commander of the SAS, to return from the desert, where his unit had successfully been conducting raids behind enemy lines. Accordingly, in early August 1942 he reported to GHQ, located at 'Grey Pillars', the five-storey block at No. 10 Tonbalat Street, in Cairo's Garden City district. Stirling was then briefed by GHQ on what it had in mind for his unit, as part of wider future operations. Meanwhile, the SAS men assembled in Kabrit at their camp, 15 miles north of Suez on the canal, during the first two weeks of August.

Stirling learnt that GHQ had planned a combined set of operations for mid-September, to cause a diversion and thus disrupt Rommel's supplies in preparation for Alexander's final offensive from El Alamein. Stirling himself may well have been partly responsible for planting the seed for the idea, by previously discussing his desire to follow up on unfinished business by staging a further raid on the shipping in Benghazi harbour. It is also certain that Lieutenant Colonel John 'Jock' Haselden had a part in fuelling the idea, for he had proposed, similarly, to lead a small-scale commando raid to breach Tobruk's defences and blow up the underground fuel storage tanks.

Haselden, a third-generation cotton merchant in Egypt prior to the war, was fluent in Italian, French and Arabic, including several Bedouin dialects, and had extensive knowledge of the local Senussi tribesmen. As an intelligence officer working for the Special Operations Executive, his official SOE moniker was 'Western Desert Liaison Officer'. He had a dark complexion and brown eyes, inherited from his Italian mother. Disguising himself as an Arab, with his hair and beard dyed, wearing robes and Arab headdress, he conducted numerous intelligence-gathering missions behind enemy lines. He won his first Military Cross in October 1941, and a month later was awarded a Bar to his MC for his part in Operation FLIPPER, the daring plan to kill or capture Rommel. A brave and inspirational leader, Haselden was selected to command the overland commando raiding party against Tobruk harbour.

However, any such initial ideas that Haselden and Stirling may have had involving small raiding parties had since been developed, by the Directorate of Military Operations, in a way in which neither of them were pleased. Conscious of the build-up of Montgomery's Eighth Army, and the imminent battle with Axis forces at El Alamein, the GHQ planners had instead developed these ideas into a vast and complex set of operations involving all three services.

The GHQ plan now envisaged the total destruction of Tobruk harbour and its fuel tanks, along with concurrent raids, including one against Benghazi harbour. The idea was to deny Rommel his Tobruk logistical supply base, for without a constant flow of fuel his long-term objective to occupy the Nile Delta could not succeed. However, this ill-fated set of operations, although bravely executed, suffered at the start from security leaks. It ranked as one of the great Allied failures of the war, ending in disaster and the death of a great many brave servicemen.

Ambassador Sir Miles Lampson invited Stirling to dinner, with Churchill, at the British Embassy, Cairo, on 8 August. It is less than clear how Stirling came to be invited to dinner in the first instance, but it is probable that Churchill's son, Randolph, planted the idea in his father's mind. Accompanying Stirling was one of his subalterns, Lieutenant Fitzroy Maclean, Queen's Own Cameron Highlanders, a former MP and Foreign Office diplomat. Other guests included the CIGS, General Sir Alan Brooke, the new C–in–C Middle East, General Sir Harold Alexander, and Field Marshal Jan Smuts. Following dinner, Churchill encouraged Stirling to discuss how the SAS role might be further developed. Stirling also took the opportunity to express the serious concern he had about the nature of the plan for the imminent raids on Tobruk and Benghazi.

Planning for the combined raids was well underway by August. In Operation AGREEMENT, the Royal Navy and Royal Marines were heavily committed to the attack against Tobruk harbour. These naval forces were reinforced with soldiers from the Argyll and Sutherland Highlanders, the Royal Northumberland Fusiliers, and specialist detachments of engineers, gunners and medics. The overland raiding component of this operation comprised the Middle East commando forces of D Squadron, 1st Special Service Regiment (SSR) and the Special Interrogation Group (SIG), a group of German-speaking Jews whose role was to infiltrate Axis lines. Carefully selected sappers, signallers and gunners also formed part of this overland raiding force. In support of the raid, the RAF was tasked to deliver the largest aerial bombardment the Middle East had yet seen.

The SAS was scheduled to concurrently raid Benghazi harbour in Operation BIGAMY, while the Sudan Defence Force was lined up to attack Jalo Oasis in Operation NICETY. The Long Range Desert Group – a desert reconnaissance unit – was also tasked to mount a diversionary raid against Barce Airfield. Of the four, only the LRDG raid, Operation CARAVAN, was successful.

Operation BIGAMY, the SAS raid on Benghazi, with its aim of blocking the harbour, sinking shipping, and destroying fuel dumps, was scheduled to take place on the night of 13/14 September. Stirling's raiding party, known as Force X, comprised some fourteen officers, and

200 other ranks. For transport they had ninety-five vehicles, including forty Ford 3-ton trucks, carrying petrol, water and supplies, with the remainder comprising mainly 'Bantam' jeeps, mounted with Vickers-K machine guns.[1] This was far from the small party raiding operation for which the SAS had been developed.

All the existing SAS troops took part, including its Free French contingent, under Commandant Georges Bergé, which had conducted parachute training in England. By this stage the unit had increased to about a 100-strong squadron-sized force, with a number of new parachutists having recently completed training. Captain George, The Lord Jellicoe, became the second in command, and Stirling arranged for the transfer of Mike Sadler from the LRDG to the SAS, as their chief navigator. They also now had a doctor with them, who had completed his parachute jumps, Captain Malcolm Pleydell.

However, the forthcoming Benghazi raid called for a 200-strong force. Some of the shortfall in numbers was made up with temporary attachments for the operation. This included two LRDG, S1 and S2 (Rhodesian), patrols under Captain John Olivey, and a Special Boat Section (SBS) detachment under Captain Mike Kealy of the Devons. A Royal Navy detachment, an RAF reconnaissance officer, and crews for two M3 Stuart light tanks to deal with enemy roadblocks and to neutralise destroyers in the port, were included. An additional fifteen drivers were also attached to the SAS, on 16 August, for the duration of the operation only.

Nonetheless, it was clear that the SAS needed to be supplemented by a number of new volunteers. Middle East Commando forces was an obvious place to seek such men. But the net was cast wider, including the Infantry Base Depot at Geneifa, and during the trawl Berneville-Claye volunteered and joined the SAS on 20 August, having evidently charmed Stirling and persuaded him of his suitability. He and a number of men like him thus essentially had to rely upon 'on-the-job training' during the long desert drive to Benghazi, for there was barely time to prepare prior to departure from Cairo, let alone conduct any SAS training. As we shall see, Berneville-Claye eventually served in the

SAS for four months, until his capture by the enemy at the end of December 1942.

Operation BIGAMY proved to be a gruelling test of endurance and fortitude for all concerned. It is therefore no surprise that a number of those involved later felt compelled to record their experiences on paper. Thus, besides official patrol reports, we are fortunate in also having a few first-hand accounts of this epic operation. Foremost amongst these memoirs are those by the SAS medical officer Malcolm James Pleydell, Carol Mather, Fitzroy Maclean, Geoffrey Gordon-Creed, and 'Jim' Almonds (written by his daughter). From these published memoirs, all of which paint an evocative picture of those early SAS days, it is possible to assemble a fair understanding of the odyssey upon which Berneville-Claye also embarked.

With Siwa Oasis now in enemy hands, Force X, with its ninety-five-strong vehicle convoy, approached Benghazi by way of a large sweep through the desert via Asyut, Kharga Oasis, the Gilf Kebir and Kufra Oasis, a total distance of some 1,600 miles. Kufra was occupied by British and French garrison troops, who had captured the oasis fort there from the Italians in 1941. Historically, the oasis had been one of a number that had linked Chad to Egypt on the ancient camel caravan route. Clusters of Arab huts surrounded the fort, and date palms and patches of cultivation bordered the turquoise-blue brackish lagoons.

For the journey from Cairo to Kufra Oasis, Stirling divided his force into three columns. Captain Blair 'Paddy' Mayne, Royal Ulster Rifles, led the advance party, setting off in mid-August, and a couple of days later Captain 'Sandy' Scratchley, a Yeomanry officer, led the main party off. The rear party was led by Captain Bill Cumper, a sapper and explosives expert, and included Captain Terence 'Jim' Chambers of the Mahratta Light Infantry, Lieutenant David Lair of US forces, and Captain Malcolm Pleydell, the medical officer.[2]

It appears that Berneville-Claye was assigned to the third party, for prominent among the NCOs in this party was Sergeant 'Gentleman Jim' Almonds, one of the 'Tobruk Four' who had operated behind enemy lines at Tobruk garrison. Sergeant Reg Seekings, a Layforce commando who had first joined the Cambridgeshire Regiment and made a name for himself as divisional heavyweight boxing champion, was also pre-eminent. Almonds recalls that Berneville-Claye did not make himself popular with the rank and file, for he did not desist from talking of the title that one day he stood to inherit from his father. Accordingly, he was nicknamed 'Lord Chuff' by the men; at the time, 'chuff' was a relatively polite soldier's moniker for the rear end.[3]

This third convoy comprised some seventy men including the Free French SAS contingent, in twenty jeeps and twenty 3-ton trucks. It departed the SAS Kabrit base around 20 August, at the stage that Berneville-Claye was formally assigned to the unit, and it carried the heavier stores. Upon reaching Kharga Oasis they realised they were in danger of not making the rendezvous at Kufra by the 3 September deadline. Thus, the party was divided into two, a slow and a fast party. The fast party included Carol Mather, Welsh Guards, two naval officers and half of the Free French, in eighteen jeeps and two 3-ton trucks. The slow party followed on in two jeeps and eighteen 3-ton trucks. It eventually took a fortnight for the third column to reach Kufra Oasis, on 1 September.[4]

Stirling personally received the BIGAMY operation instruction on 19 August and, having been detained by the GHQ planners in Cairo, he and Maclean caught up with Force X, now starting to arrive at Kufra, by flying there in a Hudson Bomber. Another officer who flew separately to the Oasis was Captain Geoff Gordon-Creed, who had won an MC in a tank battle on his very first day of action with the Royal Gloucestershire Hussars. He later won a DSO while operating with the SOE in Greece. Scratchley had recruited him for the raid to command the M3 Stuart 'Honey' light tanks. These tanks were delivered as far as Kharga by rail, from where they then proceeded to Kufra with Mayne's advance party, as he passed through Kharga.

The two Honey tanks made it as far as Kufra Oasis under their own steam, but not much further. One subsequently slid off a raised track within the Oasis and sank up to its turret in thick black mud and could not be recovered. The other blew its engine some 50 miles north of the oasis and had to be abandoned. Nonetheless, Gordon-Creed continued with the raid, and later found himself in a group which included Captain Steve Hastings, Scots Guards, and Lieutenants Carol Mather and Brian Dillon, the latter an old friend, originally of the Royal Norfolk Regiment.[5]

By early September, Kufra Oasis had become somewhat crowded, with the garrison troops stationed there now playing host to the SAS in Force X. Also encamped there was Force B, the SSR and SIG party under Haselden, for the attack upon Tobruk harbour. This force comprised fifteen officers and seventy-seven other ranks, including its LRDG Y1 (Yeomanry) patrol under Captain David Lloyd Owen of the Queen's Royal Regiment. Tragically, only several of the SSR commandos in Haselden's Force B returned from the Tobruk raid. Haselden himself was shot and killed in action, and his force all but wiped out. Only two of his commando officers, Lieutenants Tom Langton, Irish Guards, and David Russell, Scots Guards, managed with a handful of soldiers to escape across the desert to the Allied front line.

Force Z, comprising 1st Motor Battalion, the Sudan Defence Force, under Lieutenant Colonel Arthur Brown KOYLI, with attached gunners from the Sudan Artillery Regiment and Captain Anthony Hunter's LRDG Y2 (Yeomanry) patrol, was also now present for the attack upon Jalo Oasis. There too was the LRDG group, under Captain Jake Easonsmith, whose force comprised Captain Nick Wilder's T1 (New Zealand) patrol and Captain Alastair Timpson's G1 (Guards) patrol. Supported by the famous Major 'Popski' Peniakoff and two members of his 'private army', Easonsmith was selected to lead the raid on Barce airfield.

With Force X fully assembled, Stirling now for the first time briefed his soldiers on the full extent of the plan. In doing so he made use of a model of Benghazi town that had been brought in a large wooden box all the way from Cairo by Lieutenant Gordon Alston, a former commando and gunner, acting as SAS intelligence officer. The news was well received by the troops. The SAS then set about organising themselves into three parties for the approach to their assembly area, which was the Jebel Akhdar (Green Mountain) escarpment, just south of Benghazi.

Although there was a degree of reorganisation, the three parties were similar in composition to that of the three columns that had driven to Kufra Oasis from Cairo. However, Cumper now led the second party, with Stirling leading the third party, to which Scratchley also moved. We may surmise that Berneville-Claye remained with the third party, now under Stirling.

The advance party, under Mayne, consisting of five officers including Maclean and 118 other ranks, departed Kufra in three 3-tonners and seventeen jeeps on 4 September. Leading them was Captain Ken Lazarus and his LRDG S1 (Rhodesian) patrol, upon whom they relied to a large extent for navigation.

The following day, the second party, under Cumper, of six officers and seventy-three other ranks, set off in five 3-ton trucks and twelve Bantam jeeps. Then the third party, under Stirling, comprising twenty officers, including Scratchley, Pleydell, Mather and Hastings, and, one assumes, Berneville-Claye, plus thirty-five other ranks, departed the oasis the next day, in eleven 3-tonners and twenty jeeps. Mather and Hastings were assigned to rearguard duty to keep the convoy together.

By 12 September, all three parties had joined up again at Wadi Gamra, on the Jebel Akhdar scarp, their assembly area. Here, 500 miles behind the Alamein line, they were joined by Olivey's S2 (Rhodesian) LRDG patrol, which had made its separate way there from the vicinity of Siwa Oasis. Here, at Wadi Gamra, Force X was now within striking distance of Benghazi, some 40 miles north-west, across the coastal plain.[6]

The route to Jebel Akhdar from Kufra Oasis had been an ordeal, for Force X had to traverse the Sand Sea, which had been bad going for the heavily loaded trucks. From Kufra they had initially headed north-west to Zeighen, a point where the Sand Sea narrows to a 20-mile pass. From there they headed north, along the western fringe of the Sand Sea, towards Jalo Oasis. The SAS kept the oasis well to their west as they passed, for it was garrisoned by Italian troops who were in wireless communication with Benghazi and, if spotted, this would have jeopardised any hope of surprise.

Beyond Jalo Oasis, as the SAS approached the coastal airfields and thus patrolling enemy aircraft, they travelled by night only. South of Msus they then carefully crossed the Trigh-el-Abd, an old camel caravan route running west to east, from Agedabia towards Bardia, which had been strewn with enemy thermos bombs.

Given the difficult going, they fared relatively well and arrived at Jebel Akhdar confident that they had not been spotted by the enemy. However, during the trip, Warrant Officer E. Arthur Sque REME was tossed from his lorry and broke his upper femur. Pleydell was forced to amputate his leg. Moreover, one of the officers in Cumper's party, Lieutenant Commander Richard Ardley RNR, died when he was blown up by a thermos bomb while crossing the Trigh-el-Abd, finally succumbing to his serious burns on 12 September. His driver, Sergeant James Webster, Essex Regiment, was also badly injured, with a shattered leg, which Pleydell had to amputate below the knee. This was a blow, as Ardley had been Benghazi Assistant Harbour Master the previous year, when still in Allied hands, and with his specialist knowledge he had an important part to play in the planned raid.[7]

When Mayne first arrived at the assembly area, on 9 September, he met up with the 50-year-old Belgian, Captain Bob Melot, who had been dropped off a week earlier by the LRDG. Melot, who had been a First World War fighter ace and between the wars a cotton merchant in Alexandria, was now working as an intelligence officer for the SAS. Another officer, Alan Lyle-Smythe, from the Inter-Services Liaison Department (an MI6 cover name), with whom he was meant to meet, could not be found. Therefore, Mayne sent Maclean and Melot on ahead, to the northern edge of the Jebel's escarpment. From there, on the 10th, they dispatched Melot's Libyan Arab Force (LAF) assistant to Benghazi on foot, to find out what information he could.

In the interim, Melot told the SAS that he was uneasy about the operation for it seemed to him, from what he had heard, that the

Italians were expecting trouble. This was confirmed by the LAF assistant, when he arrived back a day and a half later, on the 12th, having trekked over 40 miles to the town and back. He had spent four hours there, and he reported that it was common knowledge in Benghazi that an attack was imminent, and that the Italians had thus been very busy reinforcing their defences. Even the date of the attack appeared to be known by the enemy and Arab civilians in the bazaar.

Stirling, whose party had arrived at their assembly area on 10 September, was informed of this disturbing news. He immediately contacted GHQ Middle East by wireless and enquired, given this new intelligence, whether a change of plan might be in order. Cairo responded that they held no store by such intelligence and that the attack should proceed as planned. Later, when Lyle-Smythe had also been tracked down, he also confirmed that the enemy anticipated an attack on the date planned. It seemed that the element of surprise had already been lost.

And so, with some trepidation, the following day, 13 September, Force X prepared to move out of its assembly area on its final approach march to Benghazi. A party of three officers and ten men, under Melot, set off first in the early afternoon, to take out a wireless station in a hill fort that overlooked the town and might otherwise warn the garrison of the SAS approach. Melot's attack went in as planned and his party took the fort, killing three and taking two prisoners, but one Italian managed to escape. However, Melot and Captain Chris Bailey, a new SAS volunteer from 4th Hussars, were badly wounded in the attack – the former with a fractured femur and multiple leg wounds, the latter shot through the lung. They could not be certain that the wireless station had not had time to raise the alarm.

The main force was due to attack at midnight, in the aftermath of an RAF bombardment on Benghazi, and it set off as planned in the late afternoon. But, with Melot out of action, it now had to rely on his Arab LAF assistant to guide them down the precipitous escarpment. In this role he proved less than reliable, and the SAS raiding party found its vehicles backed up in a dead-end wadi and had to retrace its steps. By the time the raiders eventually made it down to the foot of the escarpment, the RAF bombardment had stopped, and they were running some four hours late. So late, in fact, that they did not cover the coastal plain and reach Benghazi until 0430 hours on 14 September.

Accordingly, Stirling had already abandoned his original plan of attacking Benghazi from several different directions simultaneously, and instead planned to attack it just from the east, the direction from which they now approached it. Once inside the town, the force intended to break down into its component teams and tackle their assigned tasks. Having crossed the coastal plain, the SAS reached a tarmac track lined with poplar trees, which led to the town outskirts and a road barrier, at which they halted. About 150 yards further down the track was another road barrier. Both sides of the track were lined with barbed wire. It was eerily silent, and they noticed also that the earth had been disturbed on either side of the track. Cumper, the sapper explosives expert, confirmed to Stirling that it had recently been mined.

Almonds had the furthest to go to his target at the harbour mole, and so Stirling beckoned him and his team of two jeeps to drive up to the front of the column. Along with Almonds in his jeep, as gunners, were Magi McGinn, a Scot, and Fletcher, Irish Guards. The Arab guide they had with them jumped out and ran away once they had stopped next to Stirling at the first barrier. The situation they found themselves in appeared to be a classic spot for an ambush, since once committed to the narrow track beyond the first barrier, it would be extremely difficult to manoeuvre or turn around.

After a quick word with Almonds, Stirling waved to Cumper, who opened the gate and made his now famous declaration, 'Let Battle Commence'. The first two jeeps roared through, with that driven by Almonds in the lead. They were received with a withering hail of enemy machine-gun fire, and mortar shells started to land amongst the other jeeps. The first two jeeps made it as far as the second barrier but discovered it to be an impassable heavy chain across concrete bollards. With both lead jeeps now being heavily hit by incendiary shells, the crews bailed out seconds before they blew up. Almonds and

Fletcher scrambled through the barbed wire but were taken as prisoners of war later that morning, and McGinn was last seen making his way back down the track.

At the second barrier moments later was the next pair of jeeps, driven by Mayne and Chambers. Their machine-gunners lay down heavy, continuous fire against the enemy positions. Nonetheless, it became clear that they would not win the firefight against the well-protected enemy positions in their concrete sangars. Heavy fire from the other jeeps further down the track also started to suppress the enemy, but any element of surprise had been lost. With enemy reinforcements likely to arrive on the scene, and with dawn not too far off, Stirling gave the order to abort the mission; heavily outnumbered, they could not afford to be caught in the open during daylight hours.

Force X therefore beat a hasty withdrawal across the coastal plain, reaching the base of the Jebel just before daylight. During the withdrawal, Corporal Anthony Drongin, Scots Guards, was mortally wounded, shot in his hips and groin. Looking back towards Benghazi, Berneville-Claye and the other men could see that enemy aircraft were now rising like hornets from the airfields around the town. The SAS hid their vehicles as best they could in the rocky wadis, and passed an uncomfortably long day with the enemy planes circling overhead endeavouring to seek and shoot them up. Due to enemy aircraft attacks, few were able to reach their first rendezvous at the top of the escarpment until the sun had set. This rendezvous, some 20 miles from Wadi Gamra, was the stone ruins of a *zawiya* or Arabic school, marked on their maps as 'The Seat of Learning'.

After dark, the SAS came out of their hiding places and, in their surviving vehicles, made their way up the escarpment, taking their wounded to Pleydell. He was already tending to Melot and Bailey, both seriously wounded during the attack on the wireless fort, and to Corporal Doug Laird, whose arm had been broken in two places. Pleydell was kept busy throughout, for the raid resulted in several men killed, eighteen wounded and five missing. But in many respects, given the intensity of the enemy aerial attacks against them, SAS casualties were relatively few.

That night, Mather and Kealy, with five men and three jeeps, remained at the *zawiya* rendezvous to await any stragglers. The remainder headed off soon after dark to their next rendezvous at Wadi Gamra. The following day, the men camouflaged their vehicles before dawn and prepared for another uncomfortable day. As anticipated, it was not long before Berneville-Claye and the other men again saw enemy aircraft circling overhead. With Maclean was Flying Officer Laurence 'Laurie' Pyke, Royal Australian Air Force, who remarked to him that 'this is going to be a shaky do'. He could not have been more accurate, for it was another nerve-wracking day, as the enemy shot at the SAS vehicles and at anybody they saw moving.[8]

By the evening of 15 September, Force X had lost some sixty vehicles. But they calculated they had just enough jeeps, fuel and water to make it back to Jalo Oasis, where they hoped to be resupplied by the Sudan Defence Force. However, they could not take the seriously wounded with them, for they were too ill to be moved any further. French officer Lieutenant Germain Guerpillon and Driver Bill Marlow RASC had already died of their wounds. Pleydell's three medical orderlies, Shotton, 'Razor Blade' Johnson and Ritchie, thus drew straws. The latter, having drawn the short one, stayed behind with the four seriously wounded men. Leaving the wounded with one of the two Italian prisoners, who fortuitously happened to be a medical orderly, Ritchie returned to Benghazi the following morning in a jeep, under a white flag. He then asked the Italians to send a field ambulance out to collect the wounded. Bailey, Drongin, Webster and Sque were duly picked up, but it was later learnt that they had all subsequently died in Benghazi military hospital. Moreover, Ritchie died eighteen months later in a prisoner-of-war camp.[9]

Meanwhile, the remainder of Force X divided itself into two main groups, under Mayne and Major V.W. Barlow of the KSLI. A third, smaller group under Stirling waited for stragglers and brought up the rear, for at this stage Captain Arthur Duveen and sixteen other ranks were still missing. Under cover of darkness the two main groups started back on their 400-mile trip to Jalo, which took them some three days. They purposefully did not travel far that night, deciding it was better to lie up the following day in the comparative safety of the wadis at the southern base of Jebel Akhdar. However, the following night, Berneville-Claye and the rest of the men packed up their kit and headed south into the desert.

Dawn on 17 September found Barlow's party, with Sadler navigating, and which included Scratchley, Maclean and Alston, as well as Pleydell and the wounded Melot and Laird, in open desert without any natural cover. They therefore dispersed their vehicles and camouflaged them as best they could to wait out the day. Come dusk, they set off again and drove all that night and the following day.

By the afternoon of the 18th, they had reached within 25 miles of Jalo. Here they stopped, for they did not know whether the Sudan Defence Force had taken the oasis. So, leaving the rest of their party, Scratchley took a small group forward, including Maclean and Seekings, in a pair of jeeps to find out. They were gone so long that the others feared for their safety.

Consequently, on the following evening of the 19th, Captain Bill Fraser, Gordons, was sent into Jalo with two more jeeps. He returned within a couple of hours with the good news that he had contacted the Sudan Defence Force, and that Scratchley's party was safe but had found itself trapped between the SDF and Italian forces. Fraser drove back into the oasis that same evening, and returned the following morning with supplies, accompanied by Scratchley's patrol.

The Sudan Defence Force was on the outskirts of the oasis, having also received a bloody nose from an enemy that had been forewarned of its attack. Having initially taken the fort, the SDF was subsequently expelled. Now the SDF was poised to attempt to retake the fort. However, before it could do so it received radio orders from GHQ Middle East to withdraw.

The same signal confirmed that the tactical assaults in which the various raiding forces had been involved had achieved the primary strategic effect, this being to force the enemy to divert large numbers of aircraft and troops that would otherwise have been used to counter the preliminary moves of Eighth Army's forthcoming offensive. This was some consolation for all those whose raids appeared, at the tactical level, to have failed. Before withdrawing, the SDF replenished the SAS parties as they arrived, in turn, at Jalo.

Thereafter, the raiders retraced their steps, via Zeighen, to Kufra Oasis. At Zeighen, Pleydell was able to leave Melot and Laird with the Sudan Defence Force doctor, who arranged to have them flown, along with several of his own SDF wounded, to Kufra and thence to Cairo. Last to arrive back in Kufra was Stirling, who had brought up the rear to collect any stragglers.

Having arrived in Kufra, Stirling, Mayne and the majority of the original SAS officers and men flew back to Cairo in Bristol Bombays, via Wadi Halfa, where they refuelled, to refit and have available a squadron-sized force for operations as soon as possible. This group, which included Berneville-Claye, formed the basis of A Squadron, under Mayne. Indeed, Mayne was instrumental in selecting the officers and men for his squadron. By the same token, no doubt Mayne had the right of veto. Thus, it is noteworthy that in the immediate aftermath of BIGAMY, Berneville-Claye was selected to continue service with the SAS. One must also therefore conclude that his performance thus far with the SAS had been judged to be more than satisfactory.

One cannot help but wonder whether the operational codename, BIGAMY, had ever given Berneville-Claye cause for thought of his second wife, Nina – particularly in the unlawful manner by which he had married her two years previously in England.

Meanwhile, Mather and Hastings remained behind in Kufra Oasis. Then, along with Gordon-Creed, Dillon and the Free French SAS, they led the remainder of the men, including those temporarily attached for the operation only and others deemed not suitable for further SAS service, overland to Cairo. Leaving behind their remnant fleet of beaten-up vehicles, for this five-day trip they first hitched a lift with an SDF convoy of thirty 10-ton trucks to Wadi Halfa. From there they next caught a riverboat to Aswan, and then the train to Cairo.

The Benghazi raid had undoubtedly been a baptism of fire for Berneville-Claye and, for that matter, others who had joined the SAS just prior to BIGAMY. Although he did not know it at the time, for Berneville-Claye this raid was the first of three distinct and significant operations in which he was engaged while serving four months in the SAS.

Chapter 3

1st SAS Regiment – Operations LIGHTFOOT and PALMYRA

In the aftermath of BIGAMY, Berneville-Claye arrived back in Cairo, in late September 1942, and was promoted to war substantive lieutenant on 1 October.[1] Unbeknown to him he was on the cusp of deploying on the second of three major SAS operations in which he would be involved – this one being the SAS role in supporting Eighth Army's forthcoming El Alamein offensive, codenamed Operation LIGHTFOOT, planned for the night of 23/24 October.

This period was also a time of momentous change for the SAS itself, expanding in strength and being granted official regimental status within the British Army. GHQ Middle East issued the order to expand L Detachment SAS into 1st SAS Regiment on 28 September 1942, in the aftermath of the Benghazi raid. Concurrently, the Middle East commando force – the 1st Special Service Regiment (1 SSR) – was disbanded at the end of October.

The expansion of the SAS had received prime ministerial endorsement the previous month, when Stirling had dined with Churchill at the British Embassy in Cairo, on 8 August, during which he had outlined his plans for the SAS. Churchill was clearly impressed with the proposals, for the following morning he instructed his private secretary to ask Stirling to put his recommendations in writing and have them delivered later that same day. Stirling wasted no time in complying. He recommended that L Detachment SAS should be expanded in scope and role, absorbing other existing special service personnel and functions, and that the other special units should be disbanded.

Stirling was conscious that this was a far-reaching recommendation. However, by this stage he was conscious of and had experienced the 'empire-building' manoeuvrings of other military departments and the associated threats to the continued existence of his own SAS unit. Thus, he had decided to go on the offensive with a strong proposal of his own. His gambit paid off and Churchill was evidently won over, for Stirling was invited to dinner again that evening at the embassy, to discuss his proposals with the prime minister in greater detail.

Churchill conveyed his endorsement of Stirling's proposal to the new C-in-C Middle East. Accordingly, Alexander's chief of staff, Major General Richard McCreery, developed a plan in September to expand and raise the SAS to the status of a full regiment. By this stage, Director of Military Operations (DMO) had secured control of all raiding forces, from Director of Combined Operations (DCO). Thus, the newly established 1 SAS was placed under control of a newly established DMO department, General Staff (Raiding Forces). Moreover, the military hierarchy considered that this G(RF) control measure also had the benefit of curtailing Stirling's habit of routinely bypassing intermediary military command, and instead seeking an audience with the top of the hierarchy.

Operation BIGAMY in mid-September had been the first unsuccessful SAS operation since its first mission, Operation SQUATTER, the previous year. However, the ill-fated raid on Benghazi did not derail the planned expansion of the regiment, nor Stirling's future role as its commanding officer. It was accepted by GHQ that under the circumstances, with the enemy aware of the imminent Allied attack and all element of surprise lost, Stirling had taken the only sensible course open to him, by aborting the mission.

On 28 September, Lieutenant Colonel John 'Shan' Hackett, in charge of DMO's new G(RF) branch, chaired a meeting to discuss the employment of 1 SAS and its part in Eighth Army's forthcoming El Alamein offensive. With Stirling just back from the Benghazi raid, and with Operation LIGHTFOOT now less than a month away, Stirling and Hackett earnestly set to business. From the start they struck up a good working relationship, founded upon mutual respect and confidence in each other. Kabrit was confirmed as the 1 SAS headquarters location and Stirling, just 26, was promoted to lieutenant colonel to command the regiment. With an expanded regimental establishment now to fill, one of Stirling's first priorities was to seek out and recruit additional soldiers of the right calibre.

Stirling's first port of call was Syria, where 1 SSR was being disbanded and where he had his pick of the commandos. Several officers transferred, including Major Richard Lea, a gunner, who had commanded B Squadron 1 SSR, Captain J.P. Power of the Hampshires, and Lieutenants Ted Lepine of the South Staffords, and Mick Gurmin of the Buffs. Lieutenants John Tonkin, Royal Northumberland Fusiliers, and Thomas Langton, Irish Guards and one of the two surviving officers from the Tobruk raid, were also accepted, along with Peter Davis of the Queen's Royal Regiment.

Others, from A Squadron 1 SSR, included Major W.A. Knowles, a sapper, and Lieutenants Peter Wand-Tetley, Wiltshires, and David Barnby, East Yorks. All these former Army commandos, recruited to the SAS, made names for themselves – not least Wand-Tetley, who, in April the following year, transferred to the SOE and parachuted 'blind' into enemy-held Greece, winning an immediate MC for his part in a fourteen-month behind-the-lines mission to equip and train *andarte* guerrillas.

Some SSR commandos had already contrived to join the SAS some months earlier. These included Captains Harold Chevalier, an Arabic-speaking Frenchman, Bernard Schott of the General List (formerly of the King's African Rifles) and Lieutenants Gordon Alston, a gunner, and R.E. Galloway of the Royal Scots. All those officers selected by Stirling counted themselves fortunate, for many of the commandos were forced to find alternative assignments. Stirling visited 1 SRR on 14 October, but he was not the first from the SAS to visit the Middle East commandos on a recruiting drive. Major Mike Kealy of the SBS had preceded him on 10 October, and Major Peter Oldfield had interviewed and selected some thirty other ranks from 1 SSR on 24 September.

However, in his quest for men of the right calibre, Stirling, accompanied by Hackett, also paid a visit to HQ Eighth Army. At Montgomery's headquarters, just 10 miles behind the El Alamein line, Stirling briefed the general on the SAS role and how the regiment could support the coming LIGHTFOOT offensive. He also explained that he was after 150 high-calibre volunteers from amongst the regiments of Eighth Army. Stirling may have had the support of Churchill, but he failed to persuade Montgomery to release any of his men. Stirling was categorically informed that he could expect none of the general's officers and men, for the best of these were fundamental to the success of the imminent El Alamein offensive in driving Rommel and his Panzerarmee Afrika back westwards.

Although Montgomery had been forthright regarding Stirling's request, he did offer him and Hackett lunch in his mess, albeit he was detained by business and unable to join them. Both smarting somewhat from their failure to win round Montgomery, in his absence Stirling and Hackett took some small pleasure in ringing up an appreciable drinks tab on the teetotal general's mess bill.

However, their trip to the headquarters was not entirely without positive results, for they happened to bump into Montgomery's chief of staff, Brigadier 'Freddie' de Guingand, before they departed. De Guingand struck a more helpful chord than his general, and let it be known that he would keep an eye out on their behalf and help if it were at all possible. Moreover, in discussion he also touched briefly upon the impending Allied invasion of North Africa, Operation TORCH. Stirling already had ambitions to expand the SAS yet further, so this news gave him cause for thought, as TORCH might set the conditions and provide the justification to raise a second SAS battalion.

The Second Battle of El Alamein was only a couple of weeks off, and still set for the night of 23/24 October, when Stirling received his rebuttal from Montgomery. Furthermore, the general had at the time also rankled Stirling by commenting upon the failure of the SAS Benghazi raid. Stirling was acutely conscious that he had got off to a poor start with the general and was very keen to set matters right.

Fortunately, he still benefitted from the backing of Alexander and had the full support of Hackett. Nonetheless, Stirling felt compelled to establish a better relationship and reputation with Montgomery, ahead of Eighth Army's imminent LIGHTFOOT offensive.

However, although the SAS now had full regimental status, the unit was still only of squadron strength. Sufficient recruits to fill the establishment had yet to be found, and those that had been secured were still undergoing SAS training. Stirling realised that there was no option other than to make best use of the troops that he did have, and to dispatch them immediately on operations. Thus, these troops, largely L Detachment men, including Berneville-Claye who had flown back from Kufra Oasis following the Benghazi raid, were formed by Stirling into A Squadron.

Under command of Mayne, now a major, A Squadron returned to Kufra Oasis, which they reached by 13 October. On 1 October, Berneville-Claye had been promoted to 'war substantive lieutenant' and on 4 October, in the immediate aftermath of the unit's formation, he was formally gazetted to 1 SAS Regiment.[2] At Kufra the A Squadron men set up their rear supply base for their forthcoming raiding operations in support of LIGHTFOOT, which was scheduled to occur throughout the remainder of October and November.

Mayne's second in command was Captain Bill Fraser. The medical officer was Captain Pleydell, awarded an MC for his brave and selfless work on the recent Benghazi raid. He recalled several of his fellow officers in his memoir thus:

> Harry Poat [KOSB], who quickly grew an attractive Santa Claus beard; Johnny Wiseman [DCLI], who on occasions would give us lessons in European history; Sandy Wilson [Gordons], young and eager; Berneville-Claye, the incurable optimist; [Bill] MacDermott [RA], a fair-headed North Irishman; and [Edward] McDonald [West Yorks], a Scot, were among their number. Mike Sadler, who was a navigator-cum-operative, now boasted two pips [i.e. had been commissioned

as a lieutenant], while Sandy Scratchley held a sort of roving commission with us.

Sergeant 'Johnny' Rose, appointed squadron sergeant major, and Sergeant Bob Bennett, both Grenadier Guards, were prominent amongst the NCOs.[3]

To Pleydell's list of A Squadron officers one must also add Raymond Shorten of the General List, who was killed in action on 19 October, and 'Jim' Chambers, who died in hospital on 4 December, following diphtheritic infection of his ulcerated desert sores. Virginia Cowles, in her biography of Stirling, also counts amongst the A Squadron number: Bill Cumper, awarded an MC for his part in the Benghazi raid; John Marsh of the DCLI; and Douglas Kennedy, a gunner, killed in action the following month, on 20 November. Berneville-Claye is also recorded by Cowles in this reference, under his alias 'Lord Charlesworth', in the rank of lieutenant.[4]

Thus, both Pleydell and Cowles place Berneville-Claye with A Squadron during this period of operations, in support of LIGHT-FOOT. Moreover, it is evident that Pleydell recalls Berneville-Claye in a favourable light, describing him as an 'incurable optimist'. This provides something of a counterweight to the way in which Almonds remembers him during the Benghazi raid, as always going on about the aristocratic title that one day he stood to inherit, resulting in his nickname, 'Lord Chuff'.

It therefore appears that Berneville-Claye was more than capable of engendering mixed opinions. Regardless, A Squadron's desert raids during October and November, preceding, during and in the aftermath of LIGHTFOOT, represents for Berneville-Claye the second of three significant SAS operations in which he was involved.

A Squadron SAS came under command of Eighth Army on 16 October. From its rear supply base at Kufra Oasis, squadron patrols, guided by the LRDG, trekked northwards across the Great Sand Sea to their forward patrol base, closer to the coast at Fort Maddalena. From here, some 150 miles from the sea and 200 miles behind the German front line, the raiding patrols sallied forth to conduct what mayhem they could.

There were three phases to the SAS operation, in support of Eighth Army. In Phase One, several raids were planned against the Tobruk to Mersa Matruh railway line, and against the coast road and associated supply depots. During Phase Two, the squadron reorganised and resupplied itself from Kufra Oasis. Commencing on 23 October and concurrent with the main Eighth Army offensive, Phase Three involved attacks against airfields and enemy vehicles retreating along the coast road. A separate SBS party also landed by sea, with the task of blowing up supply depots and vehicle parks in the El Daba region.

Mayne organised his squadron into six separate patrols, 'A' to 'F'. Then, in the final fortnight of October, leading up to and during the Second Battle of El Alamein, his troops attacked and blew up the railway line at several locations from Tobruk in the west to Fuka in the east. A successful raid occurred at Tobruk on the night of 14/15 October. However, the Sidi Barrani raid was countered by the enemy and the patrol commander, Shorten, was killed on 19 October when his jeep overturned as he escaped across the desert, hotly pursued by the enemy.

In the aftermath of the attack on Shorten's patrol, one of the great SAS endurance marches took place. Following a firefight with the enemy, Trooper John 'Jack' Sillito, Staffordshire Yeomanry, the patrol navigator, found himself alone and on foot. He essentially had three choices. He could seek out and give himself up to an enemy patrol. He could lie up and hope the Eighth Army arrived in his area before he expired. Or he could try to march back to the Kufra patrol base in the Great Sand Sea, some 180 miles away. He decided to try to make it back to his patrol base.

Sillito was ill-equipped for such an endeavour, with just a compass and pistol, a single water bottle, but no food. Having set off, he had drunk all his water by the end of the second day, and thereafter was reduced to having to drink his own urine. His first 'way point' was the

Hatiet Etla wadi, which had been used as his patrol's last rendezvous, in which it had cached emergency rations and water. With his feet torn and bleeding, and having covered 150 miles across open desert, he reached the wadi in eight days. Fortunately for him he did not need to march any further. A passing SAS patrol picked him up and drove him the final stage to Kufra Oasis. His recovery was just as impressive, for within two weeks he was fit enough to be back on active operations.

Meanwhile, on 24 October, SAS raiding parties blew up the railway again at three places – at Fuka, at 'Piccadilly', and at a location a short way west. A similar operation took place on 26 October and, during the night of 29/30 October, a further nine successful attacks were made north-west of Sidi Aziz. These were followed, on 31 October, by a further raid at Niswel el Suf station. When his charges failed to blow up a train, Lieutenant MacDermott was so disappointed that he contrived instead to capture a railway station, with his patrol of three jeeps. Having taken as prisoner two Germans and three Italians, he proceeded to lay his demolition charges. After blowing up the station, he and his patrol cheerfully drove south, back into the desert wasteland.

So successful had these raids been that an order was then dispatched to Mayne to cease from blowing the railway up any further. Eighth Army had been successful in the Second Battle of El Alamein and, advancing westwards, was likely soon to reach Mayne's area of operations. It wanted the railway line intact for its own logistical imperatives.

While A Squadron, under Mayne, was engaged in desert operations, Stirling had remained with a small team at SAS headquarters, Kabrit, to further their regimental recruiting efforts. However, he briefly ended up in a Cairo hospital during this period, having finally succumbed to his desert sores. Nonetheless, he continued to direct and manage regimental affairs from his hospital bed.

At this stage Stirling was cheered to hear that his plan to expand the SAS was gaining traction. The powers that be had given the go-ahead to form a second SAS battalion in England, under command of his brother, Bill, also a former commando officer. Some quipped that the regiment's title stood for 'Stirling and Stirling'. In addition, it was planned that 2 SAS was to be deployed, in November, to support the Allied TORCH landings in French North-West Africa.

The Second Battle of El Alamein proved to be an emphatic success for the British and, with it, Allied fortunes turned in the North African Campaign. This represented a major turning point in the war and, with Rommel's Panzerarmee Afrika in retreat and with Eighth Army hot on his heels, it marked the beginning of the final phase of the Desert War.

Furthermore, the previous year America had entered the war, following the Japanese attack on Pearl Harbor, and joint Anglo–US forces were now poised to land in French North-West Africa. As planned, on 8 November, during Operation TORCH, these troops, including the Allied 1st Army under Lieutenant General Dwight Eisenhower, landed in Algeria and Morocco. The plan was that once the French Vichy territories of Morocco, Algeria and Tunisia had been secured, these Allied forces would then thrust east against Axis forces in the Western Desert, while Eighth Army continued to pursue Rommel westwards. Once the whole of the North African coastline was in Allied hands, the Mediterranean could be opened to Allied shipping.

In early November, A Squadron SAS conducted numerous follow-on sabotage operations in the region. The targets were enemy fuel and motor transport depots. Scratchley's patrol successfully attacked the fuel dumps at El Daba. However, finding themselves suddenly amongst Rommel's retreating forces, the patrol decided its best withdrawal route was to instead drive directly east through British lines, back to Kabrit. The Gazala airfields were also attacked again. Thereafter, in mid-November, Mayne led his raiders, Berneville-Claye amongst them, back through the Great Sand Sea to Kufra Oasis, to resupply his unit and for a few days' rest. Tragically, soon after, on 20 November, one of the A Squadron patrols drove over mines, killing the patrol commander, Kennedy, and Corporal Allan Sharman RTR.

Stirling and Hackett had ensured that Alexander and Montgomery were kept well informed of A Squadron's successful operations in the desert in support of LIGHTFOOT. Montgomery became increasingly impressed by the desert raiders and, despite a somewhat poor start to his association with Stirling, the two now began to develop a good working relationship. In fact, Montgomery with due reverence informed his colleagues that he considered 'the Boy Stirling' to be 'quite, quite mad', but that such madness had a place in a war.

With A Squadron's role in support of LIGHTFOOT successfully concluded, the SAS began to prepare for their next task. This was Operation PALMYRA, the SAS role in supporting Eighth Army's push westward to Tripoli, which was scheduled to begin in mid-December 1942. PALMYRA was Berneville-Claye's third and, as it transpired, final operation with the SAS, for it was during this period that he was captured.

Within a month of A Squadron's previous deployment, in mid-October, in support of LIGHTFOOT, Stirling and his team had managed to recruit and train a second squadron of men. This newly formed B Squadron, under Major Vivian Street of the Devons, had departed Kabrit on 20 November to join forces with A Squadron in the desert.

Stirling had decided that B Squadron should be fielded as soon as possible, even though it had not undergone full SAS training. Accordingly, he managed to convince Hackett that the remainder of the squadron's training should be conducted 'on the job'. Released from hospital, having sufficiently recovered from his desert sores, Stirling and his small regimental tactical headquarters drove with B Squadron on its journey to rendezvous with A Squadron in the desert. On the first stage of this nine-day journey, from Alexandria to Agedabia, they used the coast road, as by now it was in the hands of the British. Meanwhile, Jellicoe, second in command of 1 SAS, remained at Kabrit and continued the job of recruiting and training more SAS men.

In the interim, Mayne had relocated A Squadron's patrol base from Kufra Oasis to Bir Zelten, 160 miles south of Agheila. This

440-mile trip involved a convoy of forty jeeps, and was achieved in just thirty-six hours, which was impressive going over desert terrain. As recorded by the *SAS War Diary 1941–1945*, 'In that period, the jeep driven by 2/Lt. Lord Charlesworth [*sic*] and 2/Lt. Wiseman had nine punctures.'[5] By this stage, Berneville-Claye was in fact a substantive lieutenant. With Rommel now on the retreat, the new location provided A Squadron a better base from which to harry and maintain the pressure on the retreating Afrika Korps. Thus, it was at Bir Zelten, on 29 November, that Stirling and B Squadron, with a convoy of some ninety men, thirty jeeps and twelve 3-tonne trucks, joined A Squadron.

Hidden from enemy view in a wadi at Bir Zelten, Stirling proceeded to brief the two squadrons on their role in supporting Eighth Army's drive westward towards Tripoli, which was scheduled to commence in mid-December. The SAS supporting role, in PALMYRA, was to keep ahead of the advancing Eighth Army and cause as much disruption as possible, during December, to the retreating enemy.

The plan called for the SAS to establish two main squadron bases, each of eight jeep detachments. These detachments were scheduled to mount up to two raids each week along the 400 miles of coast road between Agheila in the east and Tripoli in the west. With each detachment comprising three to four jeeps, the plan directed that the SAS should mine the road and harass the enemy's logistical lines of communication. Raiding during the hours of darkness, the SAS would thereby force the enemy to drive in daylight so that the RAF could easily shoot them up. All such raids were carefully planned to support Eighth Army's advance, and to also deconflict with the LRDG 'Road Watch' operation along the same stretch of coast.

The western sector of coastline from Tripoli to Bouerat was allocated to B Squadron, and the eastern sector from Bouerat to Agheila to A Squadron. Benghazi, now in Allied hands, was their main supply base. With orders given and having readied themselves for operations, the two squadrons headed out from the wadi at Bir Zelten to their respective sectors.

A Squadron, under Mayne and with Berneville-Claye as one of their number, was relatively close to its sector, and was in action within a couple of days. However, the terrain was particularly tough going, and given the vehicle breakdowns, four of its jeeps and crews had to be left behind. Accordingly, Mayne ordered his men to operate as best they could from the locations in which they were left.

The Eighth Army soon advanced into A Squadron's sector and, since it was clearly counterproductive to continue to destroy the road, relatively few raids were conducted. Those that were conducted proved successful, with minimal casualties, although during the opening phase, Patrick 'Paddy' J. Allen, a gunner, was killed, on 5 December.[6]

The exploits of A Squadron and its officers during Operation PALMYRA are less well documented in war memoirs and official reports than those of B Squadron, or, for that matter, C or D Squadrons. On occasion it has been suggested that Berneville-Claye served with B Squadron during this period, perhaps because very many of the B Squadron men were killed or captured, as was he.[7] If so, then this might suggest that he transferred squadrons, after LIGHTFOOT but before PALMYRA commenced, which of course is a possibility.

Absence of any mention of Berneville-Claye in B Squadron memoirs or the official patrol reports and *The SAS War Diary 1941–1945*, in which B Squadron officers are otherwise well documented, tends to suggest that he remained with A Squadron. Moreover, Berneville-Claye evidently did not transfer to either C or D Squadrons, as he was captured before either of these two latter-formed SAS squadrons deployed from their regimental base in Kabrit to the desert.

Thus, one might reasonably assume that Berneville-Claye was with A Squadron during PALMYRA when he was later captured, in December 1942, behind enemy lines and became a prisoner of war. However, it is first worth taking a brief look at the exploits of the other three SAS squadrons, which will help set the context of this extremely frenetic period, during which time Berneville-Claye became a POW.

B Squadron enjoyed the benefit of more time than A Squadron before Eighth Army reached their sector. Owing to the difficult terrain, it only just reached its patrol base, Bir Fascia, 200 miles to the north-west of Bir Zelten, by 13 December, the day before Eighth Army's push. Stirling accompanied this less experienced squadron to its sector and remained with it for the first couple of days. But he was then required to return with Sadler to HQ Eighth Army. The squadron men found their sector extremely difficult to operate in, for it was heavily populated with untrustworthy Arabs, and the enemy were still extremely active and on the hunt for them.

B Squadron, under Vivian Street, had a few experienced officers – Gordon Alston and Carol Mather, and François Martin of the Free French. However, most were new to the SAS, and in this category were Majors Peter Oldfield, RAC and Wilfred Thesiger of the General List, later to make a name for himself as an explorer and author. Three hailed from the Rifle Brigade: Captains Philip Morris-Keating, the Hon. Pat Hore-Ruthven, and Lieutenant Anthony Hough. Others included Captain John O'Sullivan, KRRC, and Lieutenants P.J. Moloney, Royal Warwicks, and Brian Franks, Middlesex Yeomanry. Nonetheless, the squadron had with it some experienced Senior NCOs, including Reg Seekings and Ted Badger.

B Squadron's patrol base, Bir Fascia, was well sited. There was an ancient Roman rainwater cistern, and camouflage was afforded by several wadis with thorn-scrub cover. As planned, the squadron then divided itself into eight patrol detachments, each of three jeeps. During the next two weeks the detachments conducted numerous raids on their allotted sections of road. A good deal of damage was inflicted and, in an effort to counter the SAS raids, the enemy was forced to divert significant numbers of troops. However, B Squadron's success came at a very heavy cost. Many of its troops were killed or captured, with only some four officers surviving or eluding capture.

The Italian Carabinieri managed to track down Mather's patrol to a cave where they were lying up for the night. The patrol managed to escape, following a firefight. But the Carabinieri tracked them down again and Mather and his men were captured and taken as POWs. Following a mock execution, they were sent to Italy by submarine.

The three patrols, under Street, Oldfield and Hore-Ruthven, operated in the vicinity of Gheddahia to Misurata, but their raiding activity was heavily curtailed by the enemy, which tenaciously and relentlessly endeavoured to hunt them down.

Having left Stirling on 12 December at Wadi Zazemat, Hore-Ruthven and his detachment drove to their patrol base at Bir Fascia. They then headed up the Wadi Zem Zem, and later combined forces with Street's detachment at Sedada. Having left Bir Gebira on 15 December, they headed north-east. Some 20 miles from Misurata, while on the road at Bir Dufan, they encountered approximately twenty trucks. Attacking these vehicles at close quarters, they used bombs to blow them up, and left them in flames. Driving on, they then mined the road and cut the telephone wires. On 18 December, some 25 miles south of Misurata, they happened upon an enemy encampment at Tauorga, but bypassed it, for the camp was too strongly defended. The two patrols were south of Gioda by 20 December, and there also they mined the road. Nearby they attacked two tanks and four other vehicles. However, heavy fire was returned, and the patrols were forced to withdraw. In the process, Hore-Ruthven was very seriously wounded, and later died of his wounds on 24 December, in the Misurata Italian Hospital.

Hore-Ruthven's weakened patrol withdrew and, on 22 December, reached Wadi Sasu, north of Henscir el Gabu. Driving through Bir Gebira on Christmas Day, they came across the enemy, attacked a lorry, and headed back to their patrol base. But upon arriving at Bir Fascia, they found the enemy in some strength. Thus, they were forced to depart and, via Wadi Zem-Zem, managed to reach Wadi Zazemet on 30 December, where they laid up for a few days. Moving on, they again encountered the enemy on 4 January 1943, before reaching friendly lines the following day. Here they heard that the patrols of Street and Oldfield were still missing.

It transpired that Street's patrol had eventually run out of petrol and been forced to abandon their jeeps near their Bir Dufan rendezvous. Hostile Arabs then gave their position away to an Italian search party. Hopelessly outnumbered, the five men of the patrol had no choice but to surrender. However, Street was able to escape when the Italian submarine which was transferring him and other prisoners to Italy was attacked with depth charges by the Allies. He and six other POWs escaped and were rescued by a British ship. Street then managed to make it back to the SAS headquarters, Kabrit, by February 1943.

Following a series of successful raids, Oldfield was shot in the neck and captured, along with his driver, Lance Corporal Gregson, RASC. Oldfield was subsequently interrogated by none other than Rommel but gave nothing away, and later escaped from an Italian prisoner of war hospital and crossed the border to Switzerland.

The patrols of Mather and Hough were also captured, although, having been transferred to Italy by submarine, Mather managed to escape from an Italian POW camp. Later, he took part in the Allied invasion on D-Day.

The patrols of Alston and Martin proved somewhat more successful, and both managed to avoid capture. Thesiger was not officially on the SAS strength, but Stirling had taken him on attachment just before B Squadron departed for the desert. He had therefore not received any SAS training, and so was placed in a jeep with the more experienced Alston. Accompanying them in another jeep were two signallers. On 14 December, their patrol set off from its base at Bir Fascia. Having reached the road, they sought out an enemy convoy, which they proceeded to rake with machine-gun fire. Having driven off into the night, further down the road they laid mines and cut telephone lines. Later that same evening, they fired into the tents of an enemy camp with their machine guns. Returning to their patrol base before dawn, they then laid up at Bir Fascia during the day, before setting off again the next night to once again seek out and attack enemy supply columns and camps.

Over the next ten days, Alston's patrol repeated this pattern, until the enemy eventually identified the location of their patrol base. Thesiger was alone when he heard the enemy driving towards Bir

Fascia, for Alston and the two signallers had gone to collect water from the Roman cistern. So he ran quickly into the desert and hid under a blanket, covered with sand and twigs, in a slight depression in the ground. The enemy looked around the patrol base but did not discover him, nor did they spot the well-camouflaged radio jeep. Then Thesiger waited quietly for the enemy to depart and for Alston to return.

However, as the enemy departed Bir Fascia they came across Martin's patrol, which coincidentally was returning to the patrol base at that time. Attacked by an enemy superior in strength, Martin's patrol escaped into the open desert, but a few hours later made their way back to join Alston and Thesiger. Later, Alston's signallers received instructions on the radio that the two patrols and any other remnants of B Squadron should remain in the Bir Fascia vicinity. There they should await the return of Stirling and SAS reinforcements, in readiness for the next series of operations planned for January.

Meanwhile, C Squadron 1 SAS, formed from the 1 SSR commandos, had been training since November 1942 at Chekka, a small village on the Lebanese coast, some 40 miles north of Beirut. Major W.A. Knowles, with Captain J.P. Power of the Hampshires and forty other ranks, arrived at the SAS base at Kabrit in the second week of November. The main C Squadron group then left Syria in their jeeps and trucks, arriving at Kabrit on 21 December. The regiment had by now grown to a strength of some fifty-six British officers and 570 other ranks, and the war diary nominal roll of officers, many of them famous for their daring feats, is noteworthy indeed.

On 30 December, the first C Squadron patrol departed Kabrit, followed on 5 January 1943 by a larger group, under command of Major Richard Lea. Meanwhile, Lieutenant Peter Davis was instructed to remain at Kabrit with a group of some twenty soldiers to conduct parachute training. The course for this had been established the previous year by Captain Peter Warr of the East Surreys. The squadron's principal operational role in the Western Desert was to support Eighth Army's push westwards along the coast, by providing it with advance guards and flank guards, and by harassing the retreating enemy. The first, smaller, patrol did not fare well, for some time after its departure from Kabrit it was ambushed by the enemy, and all were killed or captured.[8]

The second, larger, C Squadron group, under Lea with Lieutenants Gurmin, Lepine, Tonkin and Wand-Tetley among their number, after leaving Kabrit made good time and reached the remnants of B Squadron in the Bir Fascia vicinity on 19 January. Having arrived, they resupplied the B Squadron patrols of Martin, Alston and Thesiger with fuel and rations.

Heading rapidly north-west up the coastline, C Squadron next provided, in conjunction with 11th Hussars, the advance guard to Eighth Army as it entered Tripoli on 23 January. Thereafter, the squadron remained in the desert, harassing the enemy's lines of communication to the front and flanks of the advancing Eighth Army. Having subsequently reconnoitred the southern end of the Mareth Line, the last of C Squadron's men finally returned to Kabrit on 18 March 1943, after two and a half months in the desert.

D Squadron formed up on 31 December 1942, the day after the first of C Squadron's patrols left Kabrit for the desert. Based upon the core of the fifteen officers and forty other ranks of the SBS and Ninth Army volunteers stationed in Cyprus, command of the squadron fell to George Earl Jellicoe. D Squadron's ranks were bolstered the following day, on 1 January 1943, when Alexander permitted 121 officers and men of the Greek Sacred Squadron, the 'Hieròs Lókhos', to join 1 SAS.

The Hieròs Lókhos based their fighting ethos on that of the ancient Thebans and the farewell of the wives to their warrior husbands: 'Return carrying your shield, or upon it.' Founded by Christodoulos Tsigantes in September 1942, the Greek Sacred Squadron contained carefully chosen men from the Royal Hellenic Army who had escaped from enemy-occupied Greece. With D Squadron's ranks thus suitably reinforced, on 25 January 1943 a D Squadron group left Kabrit for the desert, under Jellicoe and Tsigantes.

Stirling's Regimental recruiting efforts were therefore going well. Despite heavy losses during PALMYRA in December 1942, particularly to B Squadron, the SAS caused the Germans significant trouble and, because of their raids, tied up considerable enemy manpower. Montgomery was evidently extremely impressed, for that Christmas each of the SAS raiders received from him a bottle of whisky and 500 cigarettes. With his headquarters now in Libya, at Sirte, east of Tripoli, he believed that since the Second Battle of El Alamein the SAS raiders had done more than had any division to aid his push westwards along the North African coastline.

Berneville-Claye never received his bottle of whisky or cigarettes, for he was captured in the Tripoli area, just before Christmas. Thus, it was during the extremely frenetic period of PALMYRA, while serving with A Squadron behind enemy lines, that he became a POW. However, it was some three weeks after his capture that this event was recorded in the 1 SAS War Diary.

The following month, on 13 January 1943, the 1 SAS War Diary entry records: '2Lt D.W. St.A Berneville-Claye (Lord Charlesworth) W. Yorks, reported missing on operations in W. Desert, 23-12-42'.[9] In fact, as has been related, he had been promoted to lieutenant some three months earlier, on 1 October, and thus was no longer a second lieutenant.

Later, in 1945, Berneville-Claye declared on his 'MI9 General Questionnaire for British and American Ex-Prisoners of War' form that he was captured two days earlier than that, on 21 December 1942, in the Tripoli area.[10] Thus the exact date of his capture is a little unclear and, moreover, the circumstances surrounding it are not recorded on either document.

By this stage, at the end of 1942, it was clear that the Desert War was drawing to a close. Churchill and Roosevelt met in January 1943, at Casablanca, in a conference codenamed SYMBOL. They agreed that the Allies should first deal with the Germans in Europe, with Sicily in the Mediterranean as the next Allied objective. Thereafter, they could focus upon the Japanese in the Pacific.

The end of the Desert War was marked on 23 January 1943, when Eighth Army's advance guard entered Tripoli, and the vice governor of Libya surrendered to Montgomery. However, in French North-West Africa, Axis forces had not yet been beaten and were putting up fierce resistance in the Tunisian Campaign. So Anglo-American forces, under Eisenhower, maintained their inexorable advance against Tunis from the west. Meanwhile, Montgomery continued his advance from Tripoli and pursued Rommel from the east.

Montgomery requested SAS assistance in support of this advance westwards from Tripoli. Moreover, he asked that they help glean intelligence for him on the Mareth Line. Built by the colonial French before the war, as a precaution to keep the Italians out of Tunisia, this line was a fortified defensive link between Tripoli and Gabès. The desert raiders had become such a thorn in the side of the Germans that, by this stage, they had deployed a special company of Luftwaffe paratroopers to hunt down the SAS and LRDG.

By this stage the Italians were also employing a British traitor and 'stool pigeon', Theodore Schurch, who unfortunately proved to be extremely effective at eliciting information from recently captured SAS and LRDG soldiers. Intelligence gleaned, on strength and dispositions, was then used by the enemy to better enable them to thwart further such patrols. This, it later transpired, had been a significant factor particularly to the recent B Squadron SAS patrol losses during December 1942.

Prior to the war, in 1936, Schurch, a committed fascist, had enlisted as a private soldier in the Royal Army Service Corps, at the behest of an Italian Blackshirt that he met at a meeting of the British Union of Fascists. From the outset he worked as a spy for the Italian fascists, and he deployed as such with the RASC, first to Palestine and subsequently to Egypt. When Tobruk fell he was captured by German forces and was thus able to make himself known to the Italian intelligence chief, Colonel Mario Revetria.

Thereafter Schurch was slipped into POW cells, posing as a captured RASC officer, under his alias of Captain John Richards. Inserted thus into the POW cells and mixing freely with newly captured SAS and LRDG men, Schurch (whom we shall meet again later in this narrative) soon developed a certain knack of securing information for his Italian and German masters.

On 24 January, Stirling's legendary luck finally ran out. For that day the Luftwaffe paratroopers happened by chance, it seemed, to come across Stirling's party in a wadi, and he was captured. Incarcerated in several Italian and German POW camps, he would come across Berneville-Claye as a fellow inmate. Following numerous escape attempts, Stirling ended up being transferred to the infamous camp at Colditz Castle.

Rommel was forced, through sickness, to depart Africa's shores on 9 March, and General Hans-Jürgen von Arnim assumed command. The Allies took Tunis and Bizerta on 7 May and, with the remaining Axis forces trapped in the Cape Bon peninsula, the enemy capitulated on 13 May. The end of the Tunisian Campaign was marked by the formal surrender of Italian Field Marshal Giovanni Messe, Commander of Axis Forces in North Africa. The Allies took some 240,000 of the enemy as prisoners, a defeat that was as disastrous and costly to the Germans as Stalingrad. Thus, after three years and having finally prevailed in North Africa, the Allies were now poised for the invasion of Europe.

In the final days of the Desert War, between September 1942 and January 1943, the period during which Berneville-Claye served, the SAS conducted some forty-three successful raids behind enemy lines. Since its creation, in 1941, the SAS was credited with the destruction of 320 enemy aircraft. Following Stirling's capture, Rommel declared in a letter to his wife that the SAS caused him more damage than any other Allied unit of regimental size.

Although aspersions have been cast on Berneville-Claye's effectiveness as an officer while serving with the SAS, the issue is less than clear, one way or the other. Such a perspective might be judged as somewhat harsh, given the relatively limited evidence from which to form an objective opinion. Such a view is also likely to have been coloured by knowledge, subsequently learnt, of his behaviour both preceding and after his SAS service.

As has been related, Berneville-Claye served for four months with the SAS, prior to his capture. This was an extremely active period, with most of it spent in the field on operations. The raid on Benghazi was an extreme test of endurance and mettle for all concerned. Following the raid, when others who had not performed to the required SAS standard were returned to their units, Berneville-Claye was kept on by Stirling, to serve in the newly formed A Squadron, under Mayne. He was formally gazetted to the SAS on 4 October, having been promoted to substantive lieutenant three days earlier, and thereafter served throughout Operations LIGHTFOOT and PALMYRA, until his capture by the enemy.

Berneville-Claye was dubbed by the men with the less than flattering nickname 'Lord Chuff' on account of being a bore with respect to (untruthful) tales of his family pedigree. But he was also remembered with some affection by Pleydell, the MC-winning medical officer, who described him as an 'incurable optimist'. Although he was not one of the SAS 'star' officers, he was nonetheless kept within the fold for a gruelling four months of operations behind enemy lines. The SAS did not then, nor now, for that matter, carry passengers; everybody was expected to pull their weight. Nonetheless, in the light of his behaviour, both before and after his SAS service, it is understandable that Berneville-Claye was later shunned by former SAS colleagues when this became public knowledge.

As is evident throughout this narrative, Berneville-Claye was undoubtedly extremely talented. When he put his mind to it and, assuming he managed to keep his nose clean, he could prove himself extremely effective. Sadly, he clearly had a predisposition for finding himself on the wrong side of the law. Fortunately for Berneville-Claye it appears that he was kept so busy by the SAS that, during his time with the unit, certain of his least desirable traits had no opportunity to rise to the fore.

Thus, as regards Berneville-Claye's performance during his four months of SAS soldiering, and given the relatively sparse evidence available, devil's advocate suggests that he should perhaps be accorded the benefit of the doubt. That is not to say, in the wider context of his overall service during the war, where effective leadership and integrity are essential officer characteristics, that he was not found wanting.

Chapter 4

Prisoner of War

F ollowing Berneville-Claye's capture, he was initially processed through several POW transit camps in Italy. There is scant information regarding the circumstances of his capture. However, in the process it appears he may have been 'slightly injured' – as declared by him later, in 1945, on his 'MI9 General Questionnaire for British and American Ex-Prisoners of War' form, in response to the question of 'Were you wounded during initial capture?'[1] Set up at the beginning of the war, MI9 was responsible for communications with British POWs, exploiting intelligence gleaned from them, and also in assisting British escapers and evaders from occupied Europe. Berneville-Claye also states that later, while he was a POW, he suffered a fracture of his left leg due to sport and was incapacitated for several weeks. However, it is unclear when and where this occurred.

Somewhat surprisingly, Berneville-Claye also declares on the same MI9 questionnaire form that he was not lectured in his unit on how to behave in the event of capture, nor instructed on escape and evasion techniques. Such skills now form an integral part of SAS training and, indeed, 'SERE' (Survival, Evasion, Resistance and Escape) training is provided to all British military personnel deploying on active operations, the level of training being dependent upon operational requirement and relative risk of capture. There again, as related earlier, since joining the SAS all his training had essentially been 'on the job', with little time if any for formal instruction. By early January 1943, Berneville-Claye had been moved by his captors from North Africa to the Naval Hospital, Taranto, Italy, where he remained until the end of that month.

From Taranto, Berneville-Claye was moved to Camp PG (*Prigioniero di Guerra*: Prison of War) 75 at Bari, where he stayed for some three weeks until February. He was then moved to Camp PG 96 at Padula and remained there a further three weeks, until the end of March. Next, his captors moved him to Camp PG 38 at Poppi, located in an old monastery near Arezzo, where he was incarcerated for some three months until June. Thereafter, he was once again relocated, this time to Camp PG 47 at Modena, in the Emilia-Romagna region of northern Italy, where he remained until August 1943.

In mid-August, a fortnight before the Italian Armistice, Berneville-Claye was sent to a Hospital at Cari. In his written statement of July 1945 to the Special Investigation Branch (SIB) of the Military Police, Berneville-Claye claims to have escaped from this hospital, only to be later arrested by German forces. In fact, his statement contains claims of some six, but ultimately unsuccessful, attempts to escape while he was in Italy.[2]

Regardless of the truth or otherwise of Berneville-Claye's escape attempts while in Italy, some three months later, in the autumn of 1943, Berneville-Claye arrived at Stammlager (Stalag) VIIIB at Lamsdorf, Germany. Here he was registered as a POW, at which time a photograph was taken of him holding a chalkboard in front of his chest, with his POW number, 35300, etched in white, with the Stalag camp number, VIIIB, beneath. There were, however, inaccuracies recorded on his POW card. He was born in 1917, rather than 1919 as stated. His commission was Emergency only, rather than Regular, and there are inconsistencies in the spelling of both his name and that of his next of kin. His father's name is incorrectly listed as Mr Bernville-Clay [*sic*] of Horsforth. His father, Mr Claye, did in fact live in Little Ouseburn (while Nina, Berneville-Claye's bigamously married second wife and their son, Graeme, lived in Great Ouseburn). It is unclear to what extent Berneville-Claye himself provided or confirmed these somewhat confusing details.

Stalag camps were generally reserved for 'other ranks', i.e. warrant officers and below. Thus, in December 1943 he and the fifteen or so other officers from the Lamsdorf camp were sent to Offizierslager (Oflag) VIIIF, for officers, at Mährisch-Trübau prison camp, in Czechoslovakia. Then, in April 1944, the whole of Oflag VIIIF was moved to Brunswick, where, in time, the camp's name was changed to Oflag LXXIX (79).

Berneville-Claye's POW card records that, a couple of months after arriving in Brunswick, he was sentenced to five days 'confined to quarters' (for an offence that is now illegible). Located near the Hermann Göring aircraft engine factory, Oflag 79 had previously been the barracks of a German parachute regiment, and in due course held as many as 2,500 British and Commonwealth POW officers.

Ronald Seth, a British SOE double agent, who was infiltrated into Oflag 79 in October 1944, maintains that when Berneville-Claye arrived in Brunswick he was already a member of the British Free Corps – the BFC being the Waffen-SS unit composed entirely of renegade British and Commonwealth subjects recruited to fight for Germany against the Russians. If so, then it seems possible that it was in Lamsdorf that he was 'turned' and agreed to become a German informant. It was certainly at Lamsdorf that Berneville-Claye later claims, in his statement to the SIB, that he first heard, from an Australian sergeant, about the BFC.

In Seth's book on the BFC, he uses the pseudonym of Archibald Webster for Berneville-Claye. He maintains that his German handlers put him into the camp to spread pro-BFC propaganda, and as a 'stool pigeon' to inform upon his compatriots. In the first of these tasks, it appears that he came up short, perhaps because the task was difficult to achieve without drawing undue attention to himself. In the second of the tasks, Seth concludes that Berneville-Claye was fully complicit with the Germans. The aim, besides eliciting general information, was to compromise British officers, to make them more responsive to joining the BFC.

Seth himself had been parachuted into German-occupied Estonia, by the SOE, in the autumn of 1942. Seth, rather than the SOE, had conceived of the mission, which was codenamed Operation

BLUNDERHEAD. However, the mission was poorly planned by the SOE, proving to be a failure from the start, with none of the envisaged acts of sabotage against the Nazis coming to fruition. Seth had no support network in Estonia and, almost immediately upon landing, was captured by the Estonian militia. He was handed over to the Germans, who interrogated and imprisoned him, and sentenced him to death. However, during interrogation Seth managed to persuade the Germans that he might be an asset to them, and managed to stay his execution. Thus began Seth's career as a double agent. He owed his success and survival in large part to his supreme self-belief and agile mind, and an ability to weave the most elaborate, at times fantastical, yet plausible cover stories.

Subsequently, Seth was brought to Germany, from Paris, in mid-August 1944 by his German handler, Count Christophe Dönhoff, who worked for the Sicherheitsdienst (SD) intelligence and security service, of the Schutzstaffel (SS). By the time war had broken out, the SD, under the ruthless Reinhard Heydrich, had become so efficient that it was already competing with the Abwehr (Wehrmacht (Military) Intelligence), in supplying intelligence to the Nazi leadership.

By the summer of 1944, Dönhoff, an aristocrat from East Prussia, believed that Germany was destined to lose the war. He believed his country's best approach was therefore to seek an accommodation with Britain, using the fear of and imperative to thwart Russian communism and post-war expansionism as the issue of mutual concern and negotiation. For his part, Seth managed to gain the confidence of Dönhoff by declaring to be anti-Bolshevik (which in truth he was), and by professing to believe in German–British cooperation against the perceived Soviet menace.

Meanwhile, Seth and Dönhoff devised a plan to infiltrate Seth into a POW camp. Two cover stories were created: one for Seth to use if he was interrogated by German intelligence officers not privy to the plan; and another to tell his fellow British officer inmates.

Dönhoff had earlier made plain to Seth the consequences of double-crossing the Germans. Nonetheless, before leaving Paris,

Seth contrived to dispatch a report that found its way back to his SOE masters in London. This report was the first that SOE had heard from Seth since his capture in Estonia, and prior to its arrival they had therefore presumed that the Germans had executed him. Accordingly, SOE had listed him as killed in action. Pleased to hear that their agent, Seth, was in fact still alive, SOE nonetheless initially had to treat his report and his reappearance with serious suspicion. For it could have been that Seth had been truly 'turned' by the Germans. Or, possibly, Seth might be dead, and the man in Oflag 79 might be a German agent impersonating him. The British Security Service (MI5) remained particularly wary of these possibilities throughout. The SOE was eventually able to establish to its satisfaction Seth's loyalty to Britain, but his predisposition for embellishing facts, muddying the water, and spinning a tale made SOE's job in doing so particularly challenging.

Thus it was in early September that Dönhoff infiltrated Seth, under the cover name of Captain John de Witt, into a transit camp, Stalag XIIA, in Limburg. From here he was then moved with five other British officers to another transit camp at Hadamar, and thence to Oflag 79 in mid-October. Seth later reported that, when he first entered the camp, he did not believe that his fellow British officers paid him any undue attention. However, the Senior British Officer (SBO) in the camp, substantive captain, temporary Colonel W. Douglas E. Brown, Royal Artillery, reported that the issue was not so clear-cut. Although the SBO was privy to certain facts, for example Seth's true name, De Witt, being just a cover, and of his SOE codename, BLUNDERHEAD, he later reported that Seth drew unnecessary attention to himself with an overly elaborate cover story.

Seth maintains that some time prior to his arrival at Oflag 79, the British camp intelligence officers had started suspecting that there was an informer in the camp. Also, shortly after his arrival he became dangerously caught up in the hunt for the informer, and that some suspicion started to fall upon him. To fulfil his role as a double agent, Seth of course had to liaise with the Germans and feed them false reports, or at least reports that had no overly compromising information.

Prior to entering the camp, Dönhoff had introduced Seth to Sonderführer[3] (Warrant Officer Class II) Ackermann. Ostensibly the welfare officer, Ackermann wore Wehrmacht (armed forces) uniform, but he was actually the SS political officer. He was also the specialist interpreter for Major Werner Hoffman, the elderly Abwehr security officer. If Seth needed to report to Ackermann – who in civilian life was an academic with a doctorate in philology – then Seth would ask for piano sheet music, in the presence of other British officers. This allowed Ackermann to invite him to the Kommandantur (commandant's headquarters and camp administrative area) upon an innocent pretence. Seth could then pass on reports, verbal or written, without arousing the suspicion of his fellow British officers.

A fortnight after his arrival, Seth visited the Kommandantur for the first time, ostensibly to collect piano music. While in the corridor, waiting outside Ackermann's office, he heard voices from an adjacent office, speaking in English. A heavily accented German officer was asking an Englishman where the camp clandestine radio was hidden. Although the Englishman replied that he did not know, he said that he'd endeavour to find out and report back in a few days. Seth was then called in to Ackermann's office to speak with his contact, and so was unable to identify the British informant, but he now knew for certain that there was an informant in the camp.

During November, a certain Lieutenant Webster arrived in the camp (not to be confused with 'Archibald Webster', the pseudonym that Seth used for Berneville-Claye). Shortly thereafter Webster spoke indiscreetly to his fellow officers about Allied intentions and troop movements on the Northern Sector of the Western Front. When the Germans then removed Webster from the camp for interrogation, suspicion fell on Seth, who had been one of those present when Webster was holding forth on the Allied plans. Later, in early December, when Seth quizzed Ackermann as to the reason for Webster's transfer, Ackermann responded that Webster had been sent for further interrogation because he had interesting information. When Seth asked how this was known, Ackermann replied to him along the lines that the Germans had another British informer in Oflag 79, besides him.[4]

Shortly afterwards, the SBO placed Seth in protective custody for his own safety, insofar as he always had a British officer escort with him if he left his room. This was because some of his fellow inmates had started to suspect that he might be the informant. Some had even suggested to Brown that if this was the case then Seth should be thrown from a top-floor window, with the act disguised as a suicide.[5] Such was the dangerous path that Seth was walking as a double agent.

Of course, Brown knew more about Seth than the other British inmates, in particular that he was an SOE agent who had been sent on a mission to Estonia. But for security reasons Brown could not share such information. However, Seth had so muddied the water that Brown even had difficulty in separating fact from fiction.

Despite being under protective custody, Seth nonetheless contrived to meet with Ackermann and tell him of his predicament, highlighting that he was unable to pass messages as previously, and requested that Dönhoff be informed. Ackermann responded that the situation had indeed become awkward, and the German camp commandant was also upset because, given the increasing speculation concerning an informant, the 'other man had become frightened', adding that this 'other man' did it voluntarily.[6]

Given that Seth was clearly no longer able to continue to pass information to the Germans without further suspicion, Dönhoff began to hatch a plausible plan to have him removed from the camp. This plan was reliant upon Seth feigning deteriorating mental health. However, before Seth was moved, he was still present in Oflag 79 when the Germans removed Berneville-Claye from the camp on 26 February 1945. Just prior to this the Brunswick Gestapo had carried out a systematic search of the camp, looking for the camp clandestine radio and other equipment, while all the British prisoners were held on the parade ground. The Gestapo (Geheime Staatspolizei), the Nazi Party's Secret State Police and a sister organisation to the SD intelligence and security service of the SS, had evidently been invited to conduct the search for the radio by the camp commandant.

On 11 March, Dönhoff removed Seth from Oflag 79 and took him to the Hotel Deutches Haus, Brunswick. Here Seth also met with and was questioned by Captain Braun, a regional security officer, and Dönhoff then translated a list of information that he said had been given to the Germans by Berneville-Claye. This included, among other things, the hiding place of the camp clandestine radio, the location of a camera and film, and confirmation of the existence of a darkroom. Later, Braun responded in the affirmative when asked by Dönhoff whether Berneville-Claye was the man who had also given up Webster to the Germans.[7]

All the information on this list was new to Seth, who replied to Dönhoff that, as a consequence, he could not confirm its accuracy. Moreover, he had never seen or met Berneville-Claye, although he knew of him because, on 3 March 1945, the SBO had printed a notice with his name on camp orders. This notice read: 'I have very grave suspicions as to the relations between the Germans and Captain Berneville-Claye who was transferred by the Germans to Fallingbostel on Monday 26 February. Will anyone having any information regarding this officer report immediately to his Company Security Officer.'[8]

It seems that the Germans removed Berneville-Claye from the camp for his own safety. This was after Brown warned them that the British prisoners were planning to try him for being an informer and intended to carry out an execution if he was found guilty.

Hauptmann (Captain) Ernst Kummer (who succeeded Hoffman as Abwehr security officer at Oflag 79 at the end of February) was soon interviewed, in April 1945. In his statement, Kummer declares that Berneville-Claye was transferred 'on the orders of the Höhere Kommandierende der KGF' (Kriegsgefangene), (Higher Commander of Prisoners of War), who was in the SS.[9] Kummer was referring to SS-Obergruppenführer (Lieutenant General) Gottlob Berger who was chief of the SS-Hauptamt (Main Office) in Berlin. Berger was also responsible for SS recruiting and, since July 1944, the Chief Kriegsgefangenenwesen (KGW) (Director of POW camps and affairs).

Such was the strength of feeling amongst the British officers as to Berneville-Claye's guilt as an informant that, following his departure, the SBO arranged for a Summary of Evidence to be taken on his activities. This was addressed to the Under-Secretary of State for War, at the War Office, in April 1945, and handed over to MI5 upon Brown's repatriation to England the following month.

Of the seven witnesses who provided written statements for the Summary of Evidence, five of them were inmates of Oflag 79 at Brunswick. Two were from Stalag XIB at Fallingbostel, the other ranks' camp to which the Germans next moved Berneville-Claye.

The first of these witnesses was Major Edward Oliver, Royal Engineers, the postal officer at Oflag 79. His primary task was to cultivate the Germans with whom he had contact in his postal role, to elicit information. Over many months Oliver had been able to slowly gain the confidence of a certain Soldat Schmidt, an interpreter with a Ph.D. working on the staff at the camp, whom he had found out was anti-Nazi. On 25 February, Schmidt informed Oliver that there was a British informer within the camp, and that this man was Berneville-Claye. On the previous evening, Schmidt said he had overheard Berneville-Claye talking with Hoffman and the camp commandant, concerning the covert wireless and photographic equipment. When questioned on the matter, Schmidt responded that it did not appear that Berneville-Claye was under arrest or any form of duress, and that the conversation appeared to be friendly. Later, Schmidt confirmed the same information to Brown, the SBO.[10]

Major Philip Miles, Indian Engineers, provided a short statement. In it he highlighted that in mid-February he had cause to visit Lieutenant William Vanderson in his room, in POW House 1, and inform him that he was going to move one of their two covert cameras from their hiding place in House 2. Only after speaking with Vanderson did Miles notice that Berneville-Claye was also in the room and could well have overheard what was said.

In his statement, Vanderson, who had a role as photographer for the escape committee, confirmed the events outlined by Miles. Moreover, on 27 February, the day following Berneville-Claye's departure, there was a search of Lieutenant Colonel Sundius-Smith's room, in which one of the two cameras was hidden. Although allocated to the same room as Vanderson, Berneville-Claye had only commenced using it from mid-December 1944.

Prior to this, Berneville-Claye had been running a coffee bar in the camp, which he had called the 'Nutmeg Grater'. Because of this he became known as the 'Coffee Lord' and had become noticeably friendly with the Germans. In running the coffee bar, Berneville-Claye received a good deal of assistance from and became friendly with Hauptmann (Captain) Richard Pfuetzner, a camp official. Over time their relationship grew and took on a more personal nature. Berneville-Claye divulged to Pfuetzner that he hailed from one of England's prominent families. He also told him that, prior to the war, he had never needed to work nor would need to do so afterwards, and that his father was a high-ranking English officer of some note.

In the autumn of 1944, following an occasion when the US Army Air Force mistakenly bombed the camp, believing it to be the nearby Hermann Göring aircraft engine factory, Berneville-Claye had offered the facilities of his coffee bar to assist in the relief work. Seth suggests that it was perhaps the memory of this episode that may, initially, have blinded the British officers of the camp to the possibility of Berneville-Claye being an informant.

After Berneville-Claye had moved into Vanderson's room, he received several calls from Pfuetzner and Sonderführer (Warrant Officer Class II) Gottfried Stock, a specialist interpreter, to which Vanderson objected. German visits to the room ceased thereafter, but Berneville-Claye continued meeting them elsewhere. Also, shortly after Berneville-Claye had moved into Vanderson's room, the Gestapo arrived at the camp, on 9 January, and carried out a search of House 1 (in which Vanderson and Berneville-Claye had a room) and House 7. After being kept outside for some hours, Vanderson returned to find that his kit was the only gear in the room to have undergone a particularly thorough search. All his papers and drawings had been examined and an unexposed film that was hidden in his shaving kit had been taken.

Vanderson also highlights how during this timeframe Berneville-Claye had become slovenly and unkempt, spending a good deal of his time lying on his bed. However, on the morning of 26 February, the day that he was to leave Oflag 79, he got up early, shaved, smartened himself up, polished his boots, and dressed himself in a freshly pressed battledress suit with collar and tie. Berneville-Claye provided no explanation for this, and that afternoon he left the camp without telling his British comrades. His fellow inmates inferred from this that Berneville-Claye must have been prewarned by the Germans that they intended to move him from the camp that specific day.

Following Berneville-Claye's unexpected departure, the SBO gave orders that his remaining kit be immediately searched. Lieutenant Michael Pearse, Royal Engineers, who shared Room 13 with Vanderson and Berneville-Claye, states that in a wooden case they found a portrait of Berneville-Claye, some paintings, notebooks, and a stack of buff cards. Amongst these cards was one with a plan and pencil notes in Berneville-Claye's handwriting. The plan appeared to be of their room. It correctly showed the layout, location of the door, and five bunk beds, one of which, Vanderson's, was marked with an 'X' and annotated 'hid in mattress'. Later, all Berneville-Claye's kit was collected by the Germans, and it was noted by Pearse that it was then taken to the Kommandantur, and not to the 'cooler'. Thus, the British knew that Berneville-Claye had not been placed in solitary confinement and was being otherwise handled.

The fifth statement from Oflag 79 was provided by Brown, the SBO. He states that for some weeks prior to 25 February 1945 it had been apparent to him that information was leaking, and that their German 'contacts' had confirmed there was a British informant. On 24 February he had become aware that Berneville-Claye had been contacted directly by the Germans, rather than through his orderly room as per normal procedure, and had reported to Hoffmann, the Abwehr security officer. Afterwards, when questioned, Berneville-Claye was unable to provide a satisfactory answer as to why he had been outside the wire.

Brown's statement also confirms that Schmidt, one of their German 'contacts', had informed Oliver that, on 24 February, he had overheard Berneville-Claye discussing with Hoffman the whereabouts of hidden camera equipment and the covert wireless set. Later that same day there had been an intensive search by the Germans, albeit unfruitful, of a room in which one of the cameras had been hidden. Then, on 26 February, Berneville-Claye was again sent for by the Germans, and this time he did not return. However, before the Germans were able to collect Berneville-Claye's kit, Brown ordered that it be searched, and this was when the incriminating buff card with the plan of the room and notes was found.

Brown also states that, almost immediately following Berneville-Claye's departure, the Germans started reinforcing their camp sentry and observation posts with additional barbed wire entanglements. Brown explained that he highlighted this because there was a scheme whereby, in certain extreme scenarios, the British had plans to rush and overpower the German sentry posts. Berneville-Claye had been one of the nominated platoon commanders in this scheme and so knew of it, and Brown surmised that he had therefore also told the Germans of this scheme when he left the camp.

Upon his departure from Oflag 79, the Germans moved Berneville-Claye to Stalag XIB, at Fallingbostel, a camp primarily for other ranks but which also contained an officer compound. Berneville-Claye's POW card records that he arrived at Fallingbostel on 1 March 1945. However, where he had been for the previous couple of days since leaving Brunswick is unclear.

Pfuetzner, the Oflag 79 camp official whom Berneville-Claye had befriended and who had helped him to run the 'Nutmeg Grater', provided a statement in August 1946 to the British military authorities. In it he states that, following Berneville-Claye's departure from Oflag 79, he was instructed by his commander to seek him out on an associated matter of business. Having caught up with Berneville-Claye, he found him to be in extremely good spirits, for not only did he now have a room to himself, but he was also allowed to go out from the camp. Moreover, Berneville-Claye declared to Pfuetzner 'that he had now at last achieved a situation which was worthy of an English officer'.[11] One cannot help but wonder for what reasons Berneville-Claye had been granted such rare privileges by the German camp authorities.

The senior officer in Stalag XIB was Major William Desobry, US Army, and he provided one of two statements, by officers in this camp, for the Summary of Evidence. When Berneville-Claye arrived at Stalag XIB, Desobry was informed by him that his nickname was 'Chuff' (the unflattering moniker with which he had been dubbed while serving in the SAS). Berneville-Claye also told Desobry that he had come from Oflag 79, where he had been in solitary confinement. This, he said, was a result of having been in the SAS and thus marked out as a potential troublemaker, similarly to Lieutenant Colonel David Stirling, the SAS commanding officer.[12]

Stirling had indeed been a fellow inmate with Berneville-Claye – first in Oflag VIIIF at Mährisch-Trübau prison camp, and thereafter from April 1944 when the camp was moved to Brunswick and became known as Oflag 79, up until Stirling was moved to Oflag IV-C at Colditz Castle in August 1944. Several months later, in May 1945, Stirling provided a statement to MI5 in which he stated that he believed Berneville-Claye 'to have been more than a minor stool pigeon who acted in a fit of temper'. In forming this view, he therefore came to the same conclusion as other POW senior inmates. However, in the same statement he also suggested that Berneville-Claye was never a combatant member of the SAS and was not the type of man whom he (Stirling) would have passed for service.[13]

It is of course understandable that Stirling might perhaps wish to disown an officer whom he believed to be a collaborator and was now under investigation for treachery. But it is nonetheless either forgetful or somewhat disingenuous to suggest that Berneville-Claye was never a combatant, given his service in the SAS raid on Benghazi in September 1942, and thereafter in Paddy Mayne's A Squadron. It will be recalled that following the Benghazi raid all those deemed unfit for further SAS service were dispensed with and returned to their units. But Berneville-Claye was kept within the SAS fold, and remained an officer with the unit, for Operations LIGHTFOOT and PALMYRA, until his eventual capture in late December 1942.

The other officer, from Stalag XIB, who provided a statement for the Summary of Evidence was Major Peter Warr, originally East Surreys, then SAS, and subsequently Parachute Regiment. He confirmed that he spoke with Berneville-Claye to help check out the veracity of his story. Warr believed he recognised Berneville-Claye as having been in the SAS, in Egypt. Berneville-Claye informed him that he had arrived at Fallingbostel from a Straflager (punishment camp), where he had been confined for failing to cooperate with German interrogation. He also implied that for most of his capture he had been in trouble with the Germans for similar reasons. This, besides being untrue, also clearly contradicts what he told Desobry, in terms of having come from Oflag 79. However, Warr was unable to elicit from him the subject of such German interrogation and, although Berneville-Claye never mentioned Oflag 79 (as he had to Desobry), he mentioned that he had met with Stirling in captivity.

Berneville-Claye informed Desobry that he did not think he was scheduled to stay long in Stalag XIB, as he thought he was likely to be moved on quickly to an interrogation camp. Moreover, he said that he hailed from a Guards regiment, which of course was patently untrue. But as a result, Desobry arranged for him to meet with Regimental Sergeant Major (RSM) Lord, the camp leader, who happened to be a Guardsman.

Desobry was suspicious of Berneville-Claye from the outset, and so watched him carefully. He noticed that Berneville-Claye was able to persuade the German sentries to allow him free movement between the officers' compound and the other ranks' compound, without a pass or escort, something not normally possible for an officer. It had taken several weeks of careful negotiation, including generous bribes, before Desobry himself had been able to manage this, whereas Berneville-Claye had achieved this within two days of his arrival. Desobry became ever more suspicious of Berneville-Claye's story and of his conduct, and so asked RSM Lord to do what he could to check up on him. RSM Wickham, the British 'man of confidence' at the camp, also undertook to ask Berneville-Claye several questions about senior officers at Oflag 79. None of them were convinced – quite rightly – that Berneville-Claye had given them an accurate account of himself.

Meanwhile it was noted that Berneville-Claye was asking and probing officers for answers to questions concerning the various organisations within the camp, and any schemes that might exist, particularly to take over the camp by force. He became noticeably perturbed when Desobry was evasive in the answers that he provided. Desobry also noticed that Berneville-Claye made numerous visits to the German guards' office, and that the permanent guard in the camp seemed afraid of him and complied easily with his wishes. Although this German camp guard had previously expressed anti-Nazi opinions to other Allied inmates, he watched his words very carefully when Berneville-Clay was present.

After a week or so in the camp, Berneville-Claye announced to Desobry that he expected to be informed by the German Intelligence Officer what plans they had in store for him. Later that day, Berneville-Claye left the officers' compound in the presence of Desobry and another officer. However, upon arrival at the main gate, while the German guard escorted Desobry and the other officer to the quartermaster's store, Berneville-Claye was allowed to pass freely, without a guard, through the main gate to the commandant's office outside the perimeter wire. When Berneville-Claye returned he confirmed to Desobry that he would leave the camp later that same day but said that he did not know where to.

Berneville-Claye did indeed depart the camp later that day, at the end of the first week of March 1945. An hour or so afterwards, RSM Lord, not knowing this, came to the officers' compound to speak with

Desobry, and asked him whether a British officer had departed the camp that afternoon. Lord went on to explain that, if so, then that officer was in the employment of the SS. When Desobry questioned Lord on this, he explained that a very reliable German contact had revealed to him that when the same British officer had arrived at the camp, his German guard had handed over a sealed envelope. Tellingly, the envelope had SS markings on it, and was addressed to the commandant.

This observation by Lord was later corroborated by Kummer, the Abwehr security officer at Oflag 79, in his 1945 statement. The statement declares that Berneville-Claye was transferred to Stalag XIB 'on the orders of the Höhere Kommandierende der Kriegsgefangene' (Higher Commander of Prisoners of War). As has been related, this senior SS officer was none other than Berger, chief of the SS-Hauptamt (Main Office) in Berlin, responsible for SS recruiting, and the director of POW camps.[14]

Chapter 5

Waffen-SS and British Free Corps

Following Berneville-Claye's departure from Stalag XIB in March 1945, one of the most extraordinary episodes was his dramatic engagement the following month with the British Free Corps. During the encounter he exhorted the renegade BFC men to fight under his command against Russian forces. However, at this juncture it is first worth exploring a little of the background to the BFC men, of their journey to the Eastern Front and shortly thereafter to Templin, and thus their meeting there with Berneville-Claye.

In October 1942, John Amery had suggested to Dr Fritz Hesse, chairman of the England Committee, that a British anti-Bolshevik legion should be established. The German Foreign Ministry had set up the England Committee as a body to orchestrate policy for propaganda operations against Britain. In due course, Amery, a sociopath, was one of three British traitors who were hanged for treason or treachery following the war.

Amery's concept was that such a legion, manned with British POW volunteers, should fight on the Eastern Front, similarly to the Légion des Volontaires Français (LVF) from Vichy France. Amery's idea also had echoes of the 'Irish Brigade', established in Germany during the First World War by Sir Roger Casement. Amery, like Casement before him, subsequently met the same fate at the gallows. News of Amery's suggestion reached Hitler, who became keen on the idea.

By this stage of the war, in late 1942, Germany's military was overstretched. America was by now fully committed to the war, and Germany was experiencing significant difficulties in both North Africa and with the Soviet Union on the Eastern Front. All too conscious of the difficulties of fighting a war on two fronts, the Nazi leadership was now also considering whether it might come to terms with Britain, and how Amery might be used as an agent in such plans. Specifically, whether peace terms could be extended to Britain on the premise of denying German ambitions upon Britain and her empire, in return for an acceptance by Britain on Germany's position in Europe.

Hesse hoped that Amery, an Old Harrovian and son of a British Cabinet minister, might be instrumental in conveying tentative peace feelers, through German broadcasts, to plant the idea that Germany was ready to come to terms with Britain. In the event, Amery's broadcasts did not have the desired effect, and Britain did not respond. However, Amery's suggestion for a British legion did take root. His idea was that a nucleus of some 100 volunteers be formed and that they, in turn, should scour the POW camps for further individuals with whom to establish the force. Moreover, Amery believed that a British legion would both complement and inspire anti-Bolshevik volunteers to join other national contingents from the countries of German-occupied Europe.

On 28 December, Hesse received a missive from Hitler, who was ensconced in his *Wolfsschanze* (Wolf's Lair), in the pine forests of Rastenburg, East Prussia. It ordered him to establish an English legion and suggested that members of the British Fascist Party be at its core. Hesse commenced work on the project and, over the spring of 1943, started to put in place plans to subvert and attract British POWs to the force. Although Amery was keen to remain involved and engaged with recruiting for the force, the German authorities took it out of his hands, having decided that his efforts were better focused upon other initiatives, such as propaganda broadcasts. Thus, Amery instead joined the ranks of the established traitors, William Joyce ('Lord Haw-Haw'), Norman Baillie-Stewart and Walter Purdy, as a radio propaganda broadcaster working in Berlin.

Amery had initially suggested that the force be called the 'British Legion of St George', but this was considered to have undesirable religious overtones, and the force in due course was named the British

Berneville-Claye as a young subaltern, after Sandhurst, having been commissioned into the West Yorkshire Regiment in 1941, with his mother, Daisy Claye. *(Archive / private collection)*

Blair 'Paddy' Mayne in 1941, who, in the aftermath of the 1942 Benghazi raid, commanded A Squadron 1st SAS Regiment during Operations LIGHTFOOT and PALMYRA, prior to Berneville-Claye's capture by the enemy in late December 1942. *(IWM MH 24415)*

Above: Lieutenant Edward McDonald, as the bearded driver in the foreground of a group of heavily armed jeeps, in one of the most iconic of early SAS wartime images, January 1943. McDonald won the DCM as a sergeant in the Cameron Highlanders, was commissioned from the ranks into the West Yorkshire Regiment, and served in Paddy Mayne's A Squadron, alongside Berneville-Claye. *(IWM E 21337)*

Left: Berneville-Claye, with his POW number 35300, photographed at the POW camp, Stammlager (Stalag) VIIIB, at Lamsdorf, Germany, in the autumn of 1943. *(PRO WO 416/28/92)*

Portrait sketch of Berneville-Claye, sporting a moustache, while incarcerated as a POW. *(PRO KV 2/626)*

Ronald Seth, a British SOE double agent who was infiltrated into the POW camp, Offizierslager (Oflag) 79, at Brunswick, Germany, in October 1944 and maintained that Berneville-Claye was already an informant for the Germans by that stage. *(Archive / private collection)*

Above: John Amery, architect of the British Free Corps of the Waffen-SS, with his bigamously married third wife, Michelle Thomas, in a Milan prison courtyard in May 1945, following capture by Italian partisans near Lake Como. He was later executed for high treason. *(IWM NA 24784)*

Left: SS-Obergruppenführer (Lieutenant General) Gottlob Berger, Chief of the SS-Hauptamt (Main Office) in Berlin, responsible for SS recruiting and, from July 1944, also the Chief Kriegsgefangenenwesen (Director of POW Camps and Affairs), from whose office in Berlin Berneville-Claye received his Waffen-SS papers. *(Archive / private collection)*

SS-Obergruppenführer (Lieutenant General) Felix Steiner, the Waffen-SS corps commander to whom Berneville-Claye reported for duty, and with whom he dined in April 1945, declaring his desire to fight with the Germans against the Russians on the Eastern Front. *(Archive / private collection)*

British Free Corps soldiers of the Waffen-SS, Kenneth Berry (left) and Alfred Minchin (right), both wearing the German field-grey uniform, but with an armband on the left cuff, inscribed 'British Free Corps'; a Union Jack badge just above that; and, on the right collar, a black patch with three heraldic lions. *(PRO HO 45/25817 & HO 45/25820)*

Above left: Thomas Cooper, most sinister of the 'Big Six' of the British Free Corps, present at the formal embodiment of the BFC in January 1944, and prior to that serving with the mainstream Waffen-SS in occupied Poland, and subsequently on the Eastern Front against the Russians. (*Archive / private collection*)

Above right: 'Our Flag is Going Forward Too' – part of the recruiting literature and series of propaganda posters, designed by John Amery in April 1943 for the nascent 'British Legion of St George', later the 'British Free Corps', before the project was taken out of his hands by the German authorities and passed to the Waffen-SS. (*Archive / private collection*)

Eric Pleasants in BFC uniform. Prior to the war, he had made a living as a wrestler, a weightlifter, a circus 'strong man' act, a boxer, and as a physical training instructor. While behind bars, for disturbing the peace in Jersey, he met the criminal Eddie Chapman, later to become the British double agent 'Zigzag'. (*Archive / private collection*)

William Joyce ('Lord Haw-Haw') on a stretcher (he was shot in the thigh when arrested) being carried into a British 2nd Army hospital, May 1945, Germany. He was the only individual besides Amery to be later executed for high treason. *(IWM BU 6918)*

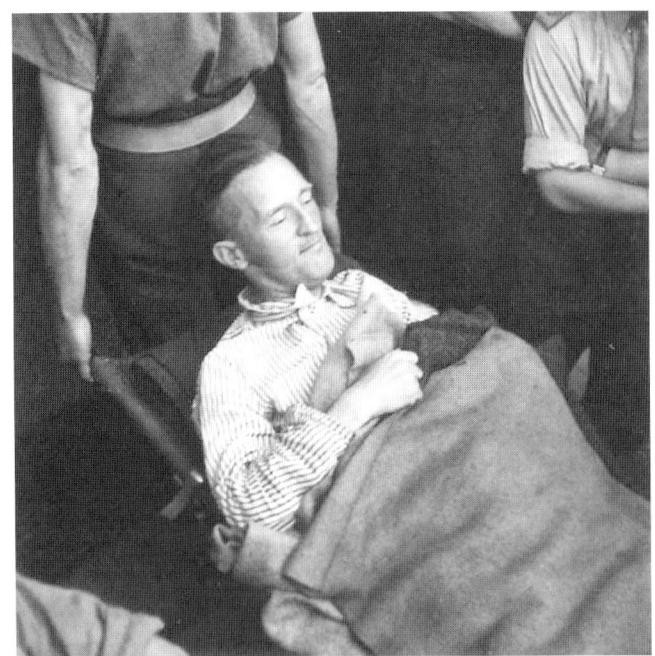

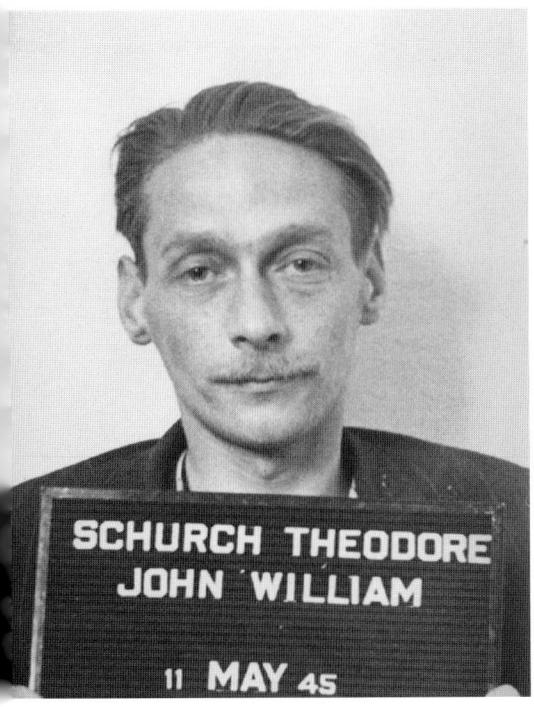

Above left: Theodore Schurch, a fascist spy who worked for the Italians and Germans and, as a 'stool pigeon', specialised in eliciting information from recently captured SAS and LRDG soldiers. He was the only soldier executed for treachery committed during the Second World War. *(PRO WO 204/13021)*

Above right: Donald Hume, holding a replica of the SS dagger with which he killed Stanley Setty, at whose trial for murder, in January 1950, Berneville-Claye was called as a surprise witness for the defence. *(Archive / Mirror Features)*

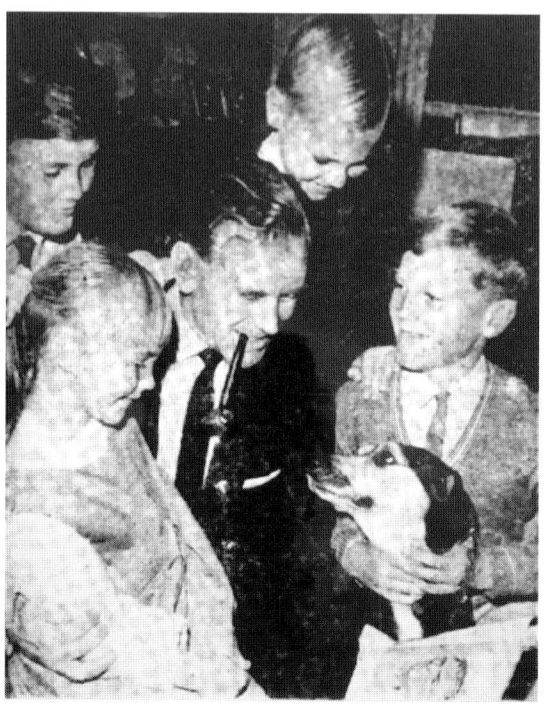

Above left: Berneville-Claye, surrounded by his family at his home in Canberra, Australia, being introduced to the city's residents, in a newspaper article on Anzac Day 1964, as a supposed war hero. *(Archive / The Canberra Times, 25 April 1964)*

Above right: Berneville-Claye during a visit to England in 1974, feeding pigeons in Trafalgar Square, London. *(Archive / private collection)*

Left: Berneville-Claye, in a portrait photograph in his mature years. *(Archive / private collection)*

Free Corps. Responsibility for the nascent legion was officially passed, in September 1943, to the Waffen-SS (the military branch of the Nazi Party's SS organisation). Specific responsibility for recruiting was given to SS-Obergruppenführer (Lieutenant General) Gottlob Berger, a close colleague of Heinrich Himmler, the SS Reichsführer. By this stage of the war all such foreign legions had been placed under Waffen-SS authority.

Waffen-SS recruiting criteria had initially been extremely strict, with members required to prove that they were 'pure Aryans'. Waffen-SS officers were expected to be a cut above their Wehrmacht counterparts and, moreover, were inculcated with the notion that they were political soldiers. Training was hard, realistic and effective, and the Waffen-SS soon developed a reputation for military efficiency and excellence. The officer responsible for establishing this training regimen was SS-Standartenführer (Colonel) Paul Hausser, a retired lieutenant general and veteran of the First World War.

In time, responsibility for training was taken on by a younger officer, Felix Steiner, also a veteran of the First World War, who later rose to the rank of lieutenant general. Training was taken a stage further. Steiner developed the Waffen-SS into what was later described as 'a force of military athletes', and he is also credited with the creation of highly effective small mobile battlegroups. The Waffen-SS soon developed a reputation for ruthless efficiency and endurance as 'shock troops' in battle, but also on occasion a less enviable reputation for war crimes. Nonetheless, by 1943, with the requirement for quantitative over qualitative expansion, the Waffen-SS could no longer claim to be an 'elite' fighting force.

Thus, by 1943, in the interests of boosting Waffen-SS numbers and in the face of competition from the Wehrmacht for 'real' German recruits ('Reichsdeutsche'), Berger came up with a novel idea. His approach was to recruit foreigners. Initially foreign recruits had to be of 'Germanic' blood, regardless of from where they hailed, but as the war progressed such strict criteria on racial purity was dropped in the interests of expediency. Thus, with an eye to expansion,

Berger initially recruited ethnic Germans ('Volksdeutsche') from across Central Europe and the Balkans, and by the end of the war in Europe some 310,000 Volksdeutsche troops were serving in the Waffen-SS.

Hitler's decision to invade the Soviet Union, subsequent to the fall of Western Europe in 1940, also had implications on earlier recruiting efforts, both for the Wehrmacht and the Waffen-SS. Himmler was authorised to expand the Waffen-SS by a further division, beyond the existing three divisions of SS-Verfügungstruppe, SS-Totenkopf and SS-Polizei, and the brigade-sized Leibstandarte Adolf Hitler (Life Guard Regiment Adolf Hitler). However, in accomplishing this, Himmler was instructed to ensure that the new division should primarily be foreign, leaving the 'Reichsdeutsche' enlistments to the Wehrmacht.

This new SS-Wiking Division was initially recruited, in 1940, from Volksdeutsche volunteers. Nevertheless, it soon became clear to Himmler that additional recruits could be secured if use was also made of National Socialists from occupied north-west European countries. In the interests of increasing its strength, the Waffen-SS and its racial theorists were content enough to accept that ethnic groups of Germanic and Nordic blood included those from Belgium, Denmark, Holland, Norway, Sweden and Switzerland. Following Germany's invasion, in June 1941, of the Soviet Union, further recruits, including right-wing anti-communists from neutral countries, keen to combat a perceived threat from the Soviet Union, were also accepted.

The narrative of a European crusade against Bolshevism soon became a key tenet of German propaganda, and Hitler formally endorsed the recruitment of 'foreign legions', to bolster Waffen-SS strength for military action on the Eastern Front. Historically, the notion of using foreign legions was very well established, with numerous examples; and even in modern times, France still retains its French Foreign Legion, and Britain its Brigade of Gurkhas from Nepal. Both the Légionnaires of France and the British Army Gurkhas have long been well established within their respective militaries, and are also widely respected, across the world, for their fighting prowess. The unifying factor for the foreign legions in the Waffen-SS tended to be a shared anti-communist stance.

Thus, from 1941, besides the SS-Wiking Division, the Wehrmacht and Waffen-SS also hosted foreign national contingents. These foreign legions, albeit with a German commanding officer, wore German uniforms but with distinctive national badges, and shared the same pay and conditions as their German military counterparts. The Wehrmacht hosted the non-Germanic LVF from Vichy France, amounting to some 6,000 troops in strength. Meanwhile, the Waffen-SS established four legions of 'Germanic' volunteers: Legion Flandern, Legion Niederlande, Legion Norwegen, and Freikorps Dänemark. Each of these foreign legions was essentially of heavy battalion strength, of at least 1,000 men, although the Legion Niederlande eventually attained 2,000 troops.

These foreign legions acquitted themselves well as fighting units on the Eastern Front, although given their relatively small size they suffered heavy casualties. Accordingly, the surviving troops from these legions were absorbed and fully integrated within the SS-Wiking Division, which was later renamed the SS-Nordland Division. Thereafter, from 1943 onwards, all foreign units were integrated within the Waffen-SS.

More recruits were to follow, and an SS Bosnian Muslim division was raised in February 1943, which fought in the Balkans against Josip Tito's partisans of Christian Serb ethnicity, for whom the Bosnian Muslims harboured an ancient hostility. There was even a Waffen-SS Free Indian Legion, some 2,000 troops in strength. Recruited from British Indian troops captured by Rommel's Afrika Korps in North Africa, their allegiance to the German cause was less concerned with anti-communism, and more an expression of a colonial struggle for independence from Britain. Indeed, after the war British authorities took a lenient stance on these Indian renegades and only a few of the ringleaders were tried by courts martial.

Of course, such a diversity of ethnicity drove a coach and horses through any notion of Aryan purity within the Waffen-SS. This ethnic *'Untermenschen'* within SS ranks was perceived by many in the Nazi Party as abhorrent, although others evidently saw it somewhat differently. Hitler no doubt viewed it as expedient and perhaps as a necessary evil. However, there were many in the Nazi Party and amongst the Waffen-SS hierarchy who had never fully bought into Hitler's view of racial purity and a Europe subjugated beneath a greater Germany, as later evidenced by the rift between the Führer and his Waffen-SS troops in the final days of the war.

By the end of the war in Europe more than half of the 900,000 troops within the Waffen-SS had been born outside Germany itself. Besides the Volksdeutsche and 'Germanic' Western European troops, there were Waffen-SS soldiers from Albania, Bosnia, Croatia, France, Hungary, India, Italy, Latvia, Lithuania, Romania, Serbia, Slovenia and Spain. Moreover, from the Soviet sphere, there were Cossacks as well as troops from Armenia, Azerbaijan, Belarus, Crimea, Estonia, Georgia, Turkmenistan and Ukraine.

Thus, this was the backdrop against which the German Foreign Office directed the Waffen-SS, in September 1943, to take responsibility for raising a British legion. Berger, the SS chief recruiter, expressed initial misgivings as to the viability of the project. This was perhaps understandable, given that earlier, initial attempts in the summer of that year to recruit for the BFC had met with little success. Conscious that British fascist and anti-Bolshevist supporters would first need to be separated from their comrades in the POW camps, the German Foreign Ministry's England Committee had set up two 'holiday' camps for prisoners. From these camps they planned to subvert and recruit British POWs.

These two 'holiday' camps were set up in the early summer, as sub-camps of Stalag IIID. The first, for officers, known as Stalag IIID (Special Detachment 999) was established in Zehlendorf. The second, for other ranks, Stalag IIID (Special Detachment 517) was in Genshagen. Nonetheless, what had ostensibly been seen as a good idea by the German authorities was subsequently poorly handled, and very few British POWs joined. Potential success was also negated by the fact that the Abwehr had selected, as their covert operative in Genshagen, a certain John Brown, a battery quartermaster in the Royal Artillery.

The Germans thought that Brown, a British fascist, was loyal to them. In fact, Brown remained loyal to Britain and, working as a double agent, thwarted German endeavours, reporting the while in coded messages to MI9. This was how MI5 came to learn so much about the BFC from the time of its inception. For this dangerous work, Brown was later awarded the Distinguished Conduct Medal.

If the 'holiday' camps at Stalag IIID had been the German 'carrot' in terms of its recruiting efforts, then the 'stick' was Stalag IIIA, a Transit and Interrogation Camp, at Luckenwalde. Here the Germans already employed a small handful of British traitors as stool pigeons and provocateurs. At Luckenwalde the Germans tried coercion and intimidation to recruit recently captured British POWs. As a result, a few disgruntled, pressed men were secured. However, in terms of recruiting for a British fighting legion, pressed men were never going to compare favourably with true volunteers. Therefore, as with the 'holiday' camps at Stalag IIID, recruiting endeavours at Stalag IIIA proved largely to be a failure.

Thus, in September 1943, with initial recruiting opportunities squandered, the Waffen-SS inherited the nascent legion, comprising just a handful of British renegades. Despite Berger's expressed misgivings, in January 1944 the legion was formally embodied as a military unit of the Waffen-SS, under the title of the British Free Corps. This, despite the case that the unit had yet to achieve platoon strength, for the German authorities were of a view that at least 'thirty soldiers' should be recruited before the BFC project could be considered viable.

Present at the BFC's formal embodiment were just a handful of British renegades, later referred to as the 'Big Six'. The most influential was Thomas Cooper. Of mixed parentage, he had travelled prior to the war, with his German mother, from London to Stuttgart to seek employment. After war broke out Cooper stayed on. Unable to join the Wehrmacht because of his British nationality, in 1940 he instead enlisted in the Waffen-SS. During 1941 he saw active service in occupied Poland, during which time he later boasted, to BFC associates, of having been involved in atrocities in the Warsaw and Krakow ghettoes. Although the evidence for such war crimes rests on hearsay, Adrian Weale comments in his book on the BFC that 'the circumstantial case is compelling'.

Subsequently, in February 1943, Cooper was in action against the Soviets on the Eastern Front, in the vicinity of Leningrad, where he was severely wounded in both legs by shrapnel. This earned him the German 'Wound Badge in Black', which was worn in his lapel, making him one of only a few Britons to have been issued a German combat decoration during the war.[1]

The other five renegades of the original 'Big Six' included Francis McLardy, a sergeant in the RAMC, captured in Belgium in May 1940. Roy Courlander, a New Zealander, captured in Greece in April 1941, who initially worked for the German 'Büro Concordia' black propaganda radio station, and Edwin Martin, a Canadian soldier, captured in August 1942 during the raid on Dieppe, also featured. Others were Alfred Minchin, a merchant seaman, taken prisoner in March 1942 after his ship, SS *Empire Ranger*, was sunk off Norway, and John Wilson, of No. 3 Commando, captured during a raid in southern Italy in October 1943.

By this stage it seems clear that every opportunity for recruits and associated propaganda potential was being explored by Germany, particularly in view of the significant military setbacks that it had experienced in 1943. These included defeat by the Russians in Stalingrad in January, victory by the Western Allies in North Africa in May, and Italy's capitulation and armistice with the Allies in September.

Accordingly, a German officer was carefully selected to command the unit. This was SS-Hauptsturmführer (Captain) Hans Roepke, who was officially designated as the 'liaison officer'. Militarily efficient and intelligent, Roepke had, prior to the war, been a law student at Berlin University and he also spoke and wrote fluent English on account of having spent a year in America as an exchange student. It was explained to the BFC men that, until a suitable renegade British officer was found, Roepke was to remain in command of them. Moreover, Wilhelm 'Bob' Rössler, a Wehrmacht interpreter, blind in one eye, was attached to the BFC.

The role of the BFC was confirmed as a fighting unit, for operations on the Eastern Front against the Soviets. It was also made clear that it would never be used against British or Commonwealth forces. Members were not required to swear an oath to Hitler, nor have their blood groups tattooed under their arms, as per standard SS practice. They were to be paid similarly to their German counterparts, in line with their rank, and they were to wear the standard German field-grey uniform, but with BFC unit insignia. It says something of German early confidence in the project that 800 sets of such insignia were made, although, in the event, the BFC never achieved even platoon strength.

In February 1944, the BFC moved from their billet in Pankow, Berlin, to the SS Haus Germanien Barracks in Hildesheim, near Hannover. Here, two months later, they received the special insignia for their uniform. This comprised: an armband worn just above the left cuff, inscribed 'British Free Corps' in Gothic-style script; a Union Jack badge worn just above that (but later worn on the right shoulder); and, on the right collar, a black patch with three heraldic lions, as on the British Royal Standard. Also worn on the left arm, just below the shoulder, was the German eagle and swastika. Around the waist of their field-grey uniform they wore the standard Waffen-SS leather belt, with the motto *'Meine Ehre heisst Treue'* (My Honour is Loyalty), and they were issued also with leather boots and gaiters, and a greatcoat and field cap.

With uniforms and insignia having been established and with side arms issued, Cooper was promoted to SS-Oberscharführer (staff sergeant). Roepke then informed the men that their priority was to recruit new members from the various Stalags, Oflags and work parties. Recruits subsequently began to trickle in, and by June 1944, BFC numbers had risen to twenty-three.

However, poor discipline amongst the BFC, and a concerted effort by one of their number, Thomas Freeman, to sabotage the corps, meant that numbers never grew appreciably thereafter. Freeman, a private in 7 Commando of Layforce, proved to be the only BFC member who was later unequivocally cleared of any guilt by MI5, having joined for the clear purpose of sabotaging the corps and escaping to the Russian lines. Several more of the BFC, the ringleader of whom was Eric Pleasants, were shortly afterwards dismissed and sent to an SS punishment camp at Bandekow, near Schwerin, for refusing to follow orders.

Prior to the outbreak of war, Pleasants, the son of a Norfolk gamekeeper, had made a living as a wrestler, a weightlifter, a circus 'strong man' act, a boxer, and as a physical training instructor. With a Diploma in Physical Education and Physiotherapy from Loughborough College, and an ambition to become an osteopath, he wrestled under the nickname 'The Panther'. He was successful enough to have made the Great Britain squad for the 1936 Berlin Olympics. At the outbreak of war, rather than enlist, Pleasants, a conscientious objector by inclination, travelled with his wife to Jersey as a Peace Pledge Union volunteer, to help with farm work. During this period, while briefly behind bars for disturbing the peace, he met the criminal Eddie Chapman, later to become the British double agent 'Zigzag'. The two struck up a friendship and Pleasants helped secure Chapman's release and, some fifteen years later, Chapman reciprocated by ghost-writing Pleasants' first memoir.

Pleasants was still in Jersey when the Germans invaded the Channel Islands on 30 June 1940. Under the occupation the only legal employment in Jersey was to work for the Germans, and Pleasants' wife left him to take up work as a housekeeper to a German officer and, so Pleasants believed, also became his lover. Pleasants had no desire to be employed by the Germans and, without any other form of work, soon fell in with a local criminal gang, nicknamed the Jersey Jackals, one of whom, John Leister, he befriended. Looting abandoned properties, they were soon caught and thrown into jail by the German authorities. Convicted, sentenced to hard labour, and dispatched to France, Pleasants and Leister managed to escape from Dijon Prison and for several months remained on the run in France.

Eventually captured, Pleasants and Leister were returned to Jersey, and subsequently transferred to Camp Ilag VIIIZ, a civilian internment camp in Kreuzberg, where they both posed as merchant seamen, to secure better rations. From there, they were moved to a POW Camp, Marlag-Milag Nord. It was at this camp, in June 1944, that Pleasants and Leister were recruited into the BFC by Minchin, accompanied by Kenneth Berry, when they were visiting the camp together on a recruiting drive. Seemingly, Pleasants and Leister joined the BFC for no other reason than they believed they might have a better time of it than in the POW camps, enjoying better rations, the absence of any hard work, relative freedom, and the company of women.

The British senior officer at Marlag-Milag Nord had made it clear to Pleasants and Leister that joining the BFC amounted to treason. Nonetheless, the two managed to justify their actions to themselves. Although Pleasants agreed with the BFC's perspective on the threat of communism posed by Russia, he apparently never had any intention of fighting with the BFC on the Eastern Front. No more intention, in fact, than he had ever had of fighting in the British Services. Thus, the two new BFC recruits accompanied Minchin and Berry back to the SS Haus Germanien Barracks to join the ranks of the other renegades.

At the barracks a portrait of Edward VIII hung on the wall, recognised by the BFC men as their true king and, at parties, toasts were drunk to the Duke of Windsor, awaiting the day when the Germans might return him to the throne. However, although the BFC may have numbered a few fanatics, the majority were misfits who were clearly more interested in getting drunk and chasing loose women in town, in their spare time.

It was becoming increasingly clear to their German handlers that, for the most part, the BFC men were paying lip service only to their military role.

For a short while it seemed that a young British officer had been found to lead the BFC. Lieutenant William Shearer, Seaforth Highlanders, was taken on by Courlander while he was trawling the POW camps for recruits. Captured in France, in 1940, Shearer had since been in a few POW camps in Germany. While in captivity he had enrolled in an accountancy course, but the stress had caused him to suffer a nervous breakdown, and he was dispatched to the Ansbach mental asylum. While incarcerated and suffering from depression, Shearer, a staunch anti-communist, volunteered to join the German Army. Thus, he came to the notice of Courlander. However, it very quickly became clear that Shearer's disturbed state of mind precluded him from assuming any BFC duties, and he also refused to wear a BFC uniform. Accordingly, Shearer was rapidly sent back to the Ansbach mental asylum for further treatment.

Starting to lose patience with the BFC, Berger decided, regardless that platoon strength had not yet been achieved, to send the BFC to the Waffen-SS Pioneer School in Dresden. By this stage, SS-Sturmbannführer Vivian Stranders was assisting Berger with BFC recruiting efforts. Stranders, who had fought for the British in the First World War, established a scheme whereby carefully selected German recruiters complemented BFC efforts. Having arrived in Dresden in October, the BFC men began their training as Assault Pioneers, prior to service on the Eastern Front. Recruiting efforts continued concurrently, albeit half-heartedly, for it was apparent that the BFC men were still far more interested in their relatively easy lifestyle, compared to previous POW existence, and any amorous diversions that could be found in town on their evenings off.

Nonetheless, by January 1945 the BFC reached its highest strength of twenty-seven, not including any German personnel. Roepke had by this stage been replaced by SS-Obersturmführer (Lieutenant) Dr Walter Kühlich, as liaison officer. Having sustained severe wounds while fighting on the Eastern Front, Kühlich had subsequently been set to work in an administrative post. This focused upon the SS foreign legions and recruitment from Denmark, Finland, Sweden and Latvia, as well as with the BFC project. He was thus familiar with his new role and upon assuming his appointment was helped, in terms of continuity, by Rössler, the BFC's interpreter.

In the interim, Pleasants and the several BFC men who had been incarcerated for two months in the SS punishment camp at Bandekow, for refusing to follow orders, were returned to the BFC fold in Dresden. They counted themselves fortunate to have finally escaped the misery of the road-making gang and the back-breaking toil in which they had been engaged. Pleasants resumed physical training responsibility for the BFC and immersed himself in heavy gym work. He was sent to Prague with another BFC soldier, William Alexander, a tough Glaswegian from the Highland Light Infantry, to represent the Waffen-SS Pioneers in a boxing competition against the SS Police. Pleasants won his fight and Alexander lost, and they are the only Britons known to have represented the Waffen-SS in a sporting competition. While in Dresden, Pleasants also began an affair with a young German SS secretary, whom he married in February the following year.

By the beginning of 1945 it was clear to German authorities that the war was all but lost. By the same token it was also evident to the BFC men that they had made a particularly poor choice in siding with the Germans, and that their days were numbered. Indeed, morale had declined steadily over the past six months, since the D-Day landings in June 1944, since when it had become increasingly clear that the Western Allies were likely to prevail. As a result, several of the renegades endeavoured to desert, but they were quickly rounded up and, following German threats, were persuaded to stay.

The BFC renegades had become increasingly anxious. Hitherto they had given scant thought to their actions, not anticipating a German defeat. But it was now clear to them that there would be a reckoning, with unpleasant consequences for them. Many had joined the BFC to escape the tedium of the POW camps, and to enjoy a better life with access to alcohol and women. But they were conscious that such reasons were unlikely to gain them any sympathy, when judged by their fellow countrymen. They were Britons serving in the uniform of the Third Reich, their country's enemy. The notion of 'traitor' and associated ramifications was now uppermost in their minds. They therefore started to construct reasons and mitigations in their defence. As became apparent at their later trials, foremost amongst these fictions were that they had joined the BFC to escape, or to gather intelligence against the Germans, or to sabotage the BFC from within.

Cooper, for his part, planned on asking Stranders to allow him to resign and be placed inside one of the Stalags, where he hoped he could submerge himself as a POW and cover the traces of his Waffen-SS membership. Instead, he was arrested by Kühlich, formally charged, and posted to the Depot of the SS-Leibstandarte Adolf Hitler, pending disciplinary action, where he served the next six months as an SS military policeman.

BFC morale was thus already at an all-time low when, on the evening of 13 February 1945, the first bombs began to rain down on Dresden. Over two days and four major air raids, heavy bombers of the RAF and US Army Air Force dropped more than 3,900 tons of high explosive and incendiary bombs on the city, creating a firestorm in which some 25,000 people perished. Amazingly, only one of the BFC men was injured. In the aftermath of the raid two BFC men took the opportunity to desert, so to prevent any further attempts the Gestapo made a mass arrest of the remaining members of the BFC.

Following their arrest, the BFC men were escorted from Dresden to Berlin on 24 February, where they waited a fortnight while arrangements were made to send them to the Oder Front. On 8 March, Kühlich gave the remaining dozen or so BFC men a choice, for in the interim another five had managed to make themselves scarce: either be sent to the front to fight Soviet forces or be incarcerated in the Drönnewitz isolation camp. Somewhat surprisingly, the former option was chosen and, with Cooper now absent, Douglas Mardon, a South

African, was promoted to SS-Unterscharführer (sergeant) and was dispatched with the BFC section to the village of Niemeck, just north-west of Berlin.

Pleasants, who, prior to the bombing of Dresden, had gone AWOL with his German fiancée, had rejoined the BFC in Berlin. However, when the BFC was deployed to the Oder Front, Pleasants contrived to stay on in Berlin, with Stranders' nascent 'Peace Camp'. During this period, he gave exhibition bouts in German officers' messes, against Max Schmeling, the former heavyweight boxing champion of the world. His friend from Jersey, Leister, also managed to avoid deployment to the front and, with forged documents, escaped to Italy with his German girlfriend, on the last train out of Berlin.

At Niemeck the BFC section underwent an intensive, four-day military refresher course at a close-combat training camp. Here, the men were issued with MP44 assault rifles, and were provided instruction on grenades, mines and explosives, as well as on the anti-tank Panzerfaust recoilless rocket-launcher. With their course completed, they were then granted two days' leave in Berlin, prior to going into action. On 15 March, the BFC boarded their truck and headed for Stettin, several hours away on the Eastern Front, where they reported to the headquarters of III (Germanic) SS-Panzer Corps.

Subject to Soviet artillery and mortar fire, the BFC waited a week in Stettin before receiving orders, on 22 March, to report to the headquarters of SS-Nordland Division, at Angermünde. Here they were attached to the division's armoured reconnaissance battalion, the 11 SS-Panzer-Aufklärunsabteilung. They were made welcome by their battalion commander, Sturmbannführer (Major) Rudolf Saalback, a winner of the Knight's Cross, for bravery.

Besides Germans and Volksdeutsche from across Europe, Saalback's unit also comprised troops from Denmark, Holland, Norway, Sweden and Switzerland. The BFC was allocated to the Battalion's 3rd Company, under command of the Swedish SS-Obersturmführer (Lieutenant) Hans-Gösta Pehrsson, who issued them an armoured personnel carrier and an amphibian jeep. The BFC then proceeded to construct protective dugout shelters within the company perimeter, in readiness for a Russian offensive.

Thus, the BFC men found themselves at Grüssow, on the Eastern Front, during the latter part of March and the first half of April 1945. When they arrived, their entire division was being held in reserve, awaiting the Soviet assault across the river Oder. The majority of the BFC men did not have a stomach for the forthcoming fight nor, as it happened, were they put to the test. For at this juncture, Cooper, their erstwhile SS leader and comrade, returned to join the BFC. By this stage he had completed his six-month stint in the SS-Leibstandarte Adolf Hitler, with which he had been working as a military policeman at the Spreenhagen Omnibus Station.[2]

Cooper, dressed in his Waffen-SS uniform, arrived at the head-quarters of III (Germanic) SS-Panzer-Corps, in Steinhöffl on the river Oder, on 11 April. That evening, SS-Obergruppenführer (Lieutenant General) Felix Steiner, the Waffen-SS corps commander, met and ordered him to accompany him the following day to visit the BFC men. It will be recalled that it was Steiner who, in the early days of the war, had also been instrumental in developing and training the Waffen-SS into a ruthlessly efficient elite corps of 'shock troops'.

During the drive to Grüssow, Cooper advised Steiner that the BFC men were not best suited to a combat role, an opinion with which Steiner was inclined to agree. Moreover, Steiner was likely considering whether committing the men to such a role might constitute a breach of international law. Thus, having met with and shaken each of the BFC men by the hand, Steiner informed them that he had decided that he intended to pull them out of the front line and instead use them in a support role. Accordingly, the band of BFC renegades were moved to corps headquarters at Templin, some 20 miles to the west of Steinhöffl. They arrived there on 16 April and were assigned to the transport company of Steiner's headquarters staff.

Short of rations, on 17 April Cooper and four of the BFC men drove to Berlin to see what they could obtain in the way of Red Cross supplies. Returning to Templin on 19 April, upon entering their billet they were surprised to see an English stranger. Described as 'about 30 years old, five feet eight inches tall and of muscular build, with blond hair and blue-grey eyes', dressed in the black uniform of an SS panzer officer, the Englishman was talking to Mardon. Having been introduced, Cooper found that he was speaking with none other than SS-Hauptsturmführer (Captain) Berneville-Claye.[3]

Chapter 6

The English Officer

At their meeting in Templin, on 19 April, Cooper and Berneville-Claye talked for a few minutes, during which time Berneville-Claye said that he had been in the SS for the past two months, although he did not divulge in what capacity. He then asked Cooper if he could be introduced to the BFC group at large, as he wished to speak with them.[1]

As related, by this stage the BFC, a band of renegades, never more than a platoon in strength and now whittled down to barely more than a dozen, had only recently arrived in Templin. For the previous four weeks they had been in Grüssow on the Eastern Front with an armoured unit, under command of the Swedish SS-Obersturmführer (Senior Lieutenant) Pehrsson. Moreover, when the BFC men first arrived on the Eastern Front, their entire division was being held in reserve, awaiting the Russian assault across the river Oder. This recent brush with front-line experience no doubt coloured the reaction of the BFC men to what Berneville-Claye then said to them.

Having been led over to the gathering of BFC renegades, Berneville-Claye addressed them all: 'I have come to talk to you boys about coming to my company.' Following this, SS-Sturmmann (Lance Corporal) Frank Axon, one of the BFC men present, asked him 'if he was a bloody Englishman or a German', to which Berneville-Claye replied, 'I have not come to discuss that bloody matter.'[2] Launching into a speech, Berneville-Claye declared that he was a Coldstream Guards officer, the son of an earl, and had come to lead them in battle against the Russians. He said that he was their new commander, that they should in future take their orders from him, and that he had at his disposal two armoured cars with which they could fight on the Eastern Front. He also assured them all that such action was supportive of Britain's cause, for their country was sure to be at war with Russia very shortly.

By this stage it appears from both Steiner's and Cooper's subsequent statements that Steiner had already made the decision not to use the BFC men in a combat role. But perhaps Steiner was still somewhat undecided as to how exactly to employ them, for, with Berneville-Claye's unexpected and dramatic arrival, and having thus finally found a British officer to lead the BFC, perhaps Steiner thought that new life might be breathed back into the unit. Or maybe Berneville-Claye was unaware that Steiner had already reassigned the BFC to a support role, and so was working purely off his own bat in urging the BFC to follow him and fight on the Russian front.

SS-Sturmmann (Lance Corporal) Harry Batchelor, one of the BFC men present, recalls that Berneville-Claye was immaculately dressed in a well-creased and spotless black SS uniform. He also recalls Berneville-Claye declaring to them that he was proud to be an officer in the Waffen-SS, the finest regiment in the world. Batchelor's description of Berneville-Claye matches perfectly: about 5 feet 7 inches in height, rather broad for his height, fresh complexion, blue eyes, clean-shaven at the time, and that he spoke with a real old-school-tie accent.[3]

However, Berneville-Claye's speech did not go down well with the BFC men, and it incensed Cooper. Having just pulled back from a position on the Eastern Front, none of the BFC were in the least bit inclined to return to it. Although Berneville-Claye bluffed on for a while, endeavouring to win them over, he soon realised that his endeavour was futile. As the Senior NCO and spokesman for the BFC men, Cooper told him in no uncertain terms that they were not going to follow him, declaring, as recalled by Axon, 'You have come to take them back into the shit after I have just got them out of it.'[4]

For this 'insubordination', Cooper was severely reprimanded by Berneville-Claye, who also later instructed Mardon (Cooper's second in command) to watch Cooper carefully. Berneville-Claye told Mardon that if Cooper was responsible for any further action that might undermine the men's morale, then he should report him to a German officer and have him arrested. Berneville-Claye departed very soon thereafter, taking another of the BFC men, SS-Sturmmann (Lance Corporal) Alexander MacKinnon, with him as his driver and batman.[5]

But how, in the first instance, had Berneville-Claye found his way to Steiner's Waffen-SS Corps headquarters? Specifically, what had transpired during the several weeks between Berneville-Claye's departure from Fallingbostel and his subsequent encounter with the BFC renegades in Templin?

Following Berneville-Claye's departure from Stalag XIB, Fallingbostel, at the end of the first week of March 1945, his movements over the next four weeks appear somewhat sketchy. Berneville-Claye later declares in his statement to the SIB of the Military Police, in July 1945, that he was taken to a civilian concentration camp between Templin and Eberswalde, where he remained for about a week. However, even if this were the case it still only partially explains his whereabouts in that four-week period.

MI5 were later able to establish that Berneville-Claye was in the vicinity of Fallingbostel some four weeks later, on 6 and 7 April 1945. The British double agent Seth maintains, in his book on the BFC, that during the preceding four-week period, after leaving Stalag XIB, the SS sent Berneville-Claye to Berlin, where they provided him with an office job.

It will be recalled that Seth was himself sprung from Oflag 79, on 11 March, just a fortnight after Berneville-Claye. Thereafter, Seth travelled with his German handler to Berlin and remained at Dönhoff's house there until 3 April. Seth's sojourn in Berlin therefore overlapped with Berneville-Claye's time in the city. Given that Dönhoff worked for the SD intelligence service of the SS and was privy to such information, this no doubt is why Seth was confident in being able to confirm Berneville-Claye's location and associated SS activity during this period.

For his part, on 12 April the Germans subsequently infiltrated Seth across the border into Switzerland, via the principality of

Liechtenstein. The main object of this mission was to courier a peace proposal from the SS leadership to Churchill. However, the Germans did not place all their bets on Seth in this, their desperate and final diplomatic endeavour to end the war on more favourable terms. They also took care to dispatch essentially the same proposal with another courier, Lieutenant John Boucicault de Suffield Calthrop, of the Royal Sussex Regiment.[6]

Calthrop, also an inmate of Oflag 79 since 23 August the previous year, was sprung from there by the Germans on 19 March – one week after Seth left the camp – and reached Berlin on 24 March. It is clear from their subsequent reports to MI5 that, while preparing to cross the Swiss frontier, Seth and Calthrop both independently became aware, through overheard German conversations, that each of them was not alone in their respective endeavours.

Both Seth and Calthrop were subjected to some delay, while the Germans finalised plans to infiltrate each of them, separately, across the border. Each officer had a similar cover story, in that they were escaped POWs. Both these controversial agents surmised who the other might be. A degree of very unhealthy rivalry then developed between them, as each vied with the other to be preeminent in delivering to the British Government and its intelligence services the latest German diplomatic overtures.

Calthrop endeavoured to tarnish Seth by reporting that 'De Witt [Seth's cover name in Oflag 79] was a shady character, who had been put under close arrest by the SBO at Brunswick on the suspicion of having given information to the Germans'. For his part, Seth endeavoured to discredit Calthrop by declaring that he 'looked unusually well for an escaped prisoner; that his description tallied with that of Berneville-Claye', as previously described to him.[7] Of course, Seth had never seen Berneville-Claye, who was still in Germany, and so was able to suggest this with impunity, in an effort to cast aspersions and steal a march on Calthrop, whom he feared might steal his thunder.

Calthrop's high-level handler was none other than Berger himself, who suggested that once in England Calthrop should also stand for

Parliament on a platform of British reconciliation with Germany, against Soviet post-war expansion. In the event, owing to Berger's patronage, precedence was given to Calthrop, who was slipped into Switzerland the day before Seth. However, both arrived at the British Legation in Bern on 13 April, each with their respective (but similar) messages from the German SS hierarchy. After the war, for his part, Seth became an author of travel books and of espionage and, under the pseudonym of Robert Chartham, also a sexologist and author of books on sex.

Meanwhile, Berneville-Claye was seen in Fallingbostel on 6 and 7 April. MI5 was later able to place him there on those dates, having received intelligence from a contact, Willi Dederichs, who came across him at the Fallingbostel troops' cinema. Dederichs was friendly with the cinema manager, Asu, whose house he often visited following the end of a film show. Both these men provided written statements to MI5 concerning Berneville-Claye's whereabouts.[8]

In his statement Dederichs confirms that in early April, following a film show, he had gone to the house of his friend, Asu, an Estonian, who lived there with his wife and daughter. Upon entering he was astonished to see a British captain, in battledress, who had in his possession a pass, signed and stamped by a high-ranking SS Führer from Brunswick, allowing him liberty in the area. The captain had apparently wanted to enter the cinema, but Asu had persuaded him instead to return to his house.

During conversation the captain told Dederichs and Asu that he had been taken prisoner in the Dieppe raid, and that he had since become a major of an English legion (i.e. the BFC) of an SS division, raised to fight the Russians. The captain also said that his family belonged to the nobility, and that his brother was a duke who had lost an arm in the war and so now worked in London on the General Staff, in the rank of major. Moreover, he went on to express concern that if the Russians were to gain pre-eminence following the war, then his family estates and possessions might be forfeited.

The following evening, the captain visited the cinema again, but this time wearing the German uniform of a Hauptmann (captain) of the Panzerjäger (tank corps). Dederichs commented that it was not clear whether the captain had ever been in a British tank regiment. However, the captain provided both him and the three members of the Asu family with 'safeguard notes', stressing to British forces that every courtesy should be provided. These notes, written in English and in Berneville-Claye's handwriting, were signed with his characteristic signature.

That same evening, Dederichs escorted the captain back to his quarters in the Officers' Block, and noticed that all his kit was packed, in readiness for a departure the following day, apparently to Munsterlager. The captain also informed him that he had previously lived in private accommodation with a *Rechtsanwalt* (lawyer) in Brunswick, the town from where he had received his pass from the SS.

Dederichs did not see the captain again, but later surrendered his 'safeguard note' to a British NCO at a POW camp in Weeze. In his statement, Dederichs also provided a detailed description of the captain, stating that he would recognise him again. When later shown a photograph of Berneville-Claye, he confirmed that it was indeed the same captain he had met in Fallingbostel. MI5 evidently held their contact, Dederichs, in high regard, declaring him to be a 'very steady, reliable and discreet man', and highlighted that the information he gave on Berneville-Claye was echoed by Asu.[9]

Indeed, it was corroborated, for Johann 'Jok' Asu also confirmed that one evening at the end of the first week of April 1945 he saw an Englishman dressed in the uniform of a British captain, in front of the troops' cinema, reading the film advertisements. And thus he, Asu, escorted him to the cash desk of the cinema, of which he was manager, and introduced him to his wife. The captain said that they should not be alarmed, for he was entitled to move about freely and had papers, stamped by the German military authorities, which he showed to them. As it was cold and raining outside, Asu invited him into the office. The captain then proceeded to inform them that he was on the cusp of travelling to Berlin, where he would receive the German uniform of a major, and from where he'd then proceed onwards to fight. Moreover, the captain explained that he was the son of a grand duke, and that he had been a POW in Brunswick for two years.[10]

Asu also confirmed that the following evening the Englishman visited him again, this time wearing the uniform of a German captain, and explained that he was going to fight with the Germans against the Russians. He then handed Asu a 'safeguard note', which he said should be shown to the British if, during the occupation, his family were in danger and required assistance. This 'safeguard note', dated 7 April 1945 and signed by Berneville-Claye (a copy of which is in his MI5 file), states: 'Please give the bearer, Johann Asu, every courtesy for reasons for which I am personally answerable.'

Berneville-Claye's activities over the following fortnight are, once again, somewhat unclear. However, continued employment by the SS-Hauptamt (Main Office) in Berlin, as Seth suggests, appears to be likely – particularly in view of Berneville-Claye's subsequent and dramatic encounter with the BFC in Templin, on 19 April 1945. Just prior to this, as explained to Steiner's Waffen-SS headquarters, he had come directly from the SS Depot, Berlin, and shown his SS papers demonstrating this.

When Steiner was tracked down after the war he provided MI5 with a statement, in February 1946, in which it is apparent that Berneville-Claye, whom he refers to as 'the English officer', made quite an impression on him. Steiner appears to have been won over by his charm, self-confidence and quick wit, although it is clear he viewed Berneville-Claye more as a daredevil than an experienced professional soldier.

Steiner confirms the arrival of Berneville-Claye at his headquarters in Steinhöffl on the river Oder, in April 1945. Steiner's corps adjutant, SS-Obersturmbannführer (Lieutenant Colonel) Dr Franz Riedweg, confirmed that the officer's papers had been examined thoroughly and were in order, and that he had come from the SS Depot in Berlin. After the war, Riedweg, a renegade Swiss doctor, was tried in absentia by the Swiss Federal Criminal Court and sentenced to sixteen years in prison for treason.

At the time of his arrival, Berneville-Claye was wearing a German captain's field-grey uniform. Steiner duly met with Berneville-Claye, describing him accurately as a man of about 27 years of age, medium height, and muscular build, with blue eyes and fair hair. His spoken English is described as 'cultured Oxford', and he understood German very well, and spoke it reasonably.[11]

Berneville-Claye informed Steiner that he belonged to a paratrooper battalion of the Coldstream Guards, and that he had been a POW in Brunswick, where he had requested German permission to volunteer to fight on the front line. Accordingly, he had been sent to the SS Depot, Berlin, and there reported to the commanding officer. This was Berger, the high-ranking Waffen-SS officer who headed Berlin's main SS office, who also had POW camp responsibility. Thus, it was from Berger that Berneville-Claye received the authorisation to fight for Germany and the necessary SS papers.

It will be recalled that Berger, a veteran, and winner of the Iron Cross in the First World War, had been given recruiting responsibility for the BFC when, in September 1943, formal responsibility for the corps was passed to the Waffen-SS. Indeed, earlier in January 1940, it had also been Berger who had enlisted Cooper, while holding overall recruiting responsibility for the Waffen-SS. Unlike the latter BFC men, Cooper was inducted into the mainstream Waffen-SS, and as such had his blood group tattooed under his left arm. Following the war, Berger stood trial at Nuremberg for war crimes and was sentenced to twenty-five years' imprisonment (subsequently reduced to ten years). However, he was released after serving six and a half years in prison.

Having heard, during his time at the SS Depot, that armoured units of the Waffen-SS were positioned north-east of Berlin, Berneville-Claye had requested that he be dispatched there. Thus, Berger had sent him to Steiner's headquarters.

When questioned by Steiner as to why he had come over to the side of the Germans, Berneville-Claye said he was anti-Bolshevist, and felt not only English but also European. Steiner challenged him, suggesting that the British prime minister was unlikely to share his views. But Berneville-Claye countered, claiming that he knew Churchill well enough to judge him and that, along with Anthony Eden and Duff Cooper, they were every bit as anti-Bolshevist as Steiner and himself.

In a subsequent conversation with Steiner, Berneville-Claye claimed that he was distantly related to a nephew of Churchill, so had a clear understanding of the anti-Soviet views of such circles. Nonetheless, Steiner was not entirely convinced that his story entirely added up. Therefore, he asked his staff to check his papers once again, which were indeed found to be in order. Intrigued, Steiner invited Berneville-Claye to dinner that same evening.

Over dinner, Steiner conversed at length with Berneville-Claye, who, as a guest, was seated to his immediate right. Berneville-Claye had changed for dinner and was now dressed in the black uniform of the Waffen-SS armoured corps. This prompted Steiner to jokingly ask him whether he could be a paratrooper as well as a tank man, to which Berneville-Claye's rejoinder, in the same jocular fashion, was that he could learn. When asked why he had sought out to join his SS panzer formation, Berneville-Claye parried with a rhetorical question of his own, responding: 'For which unit, other than a German elite formation, could a member of a British Guards Regiment volunteer, if he should decide to do so?'

When asked by Steiner whether he would like to go up to Templin the following day, and meet there the BFC men, Berneville-Claye responded in the affirmative. After dinner Steiner asked a couple of his staff for their impressions of the young English officer, who during the evening had also managed to divulge that he was of noble birth and was the second son of a duke. They all found him to have been a pleasant, witty young man and good company, and it is evident that Berneville-Claye had worked his charm, although it seems they remained still somewhat wary of him.

The following evening Steiner met again with Berneville-Claye and asked how his visit to Templin that day had been. Steiner thought that his response was somewhat absent-minded. But nonetheless,

Berneville-Claye confirmed that he had indeed spoken with the BFC men, although he did not rate the sergeant highly. No doubt this remark was because of his heated dispute with Cooper.

Steiner informed Berneville-Claye that, upon reflection, he was not inclined to use him and the BFC men in a combat role. Steiner was somewhat surprised at Berneville-Claye's apparent willingness to accept this change, given his earlier avowed desire to fight at the front. Steiner mentioned this to his corps adjutant, Riedweg, who said that he had also thought similarly, and so had put it to Berneville-Claye that he might be in the Intelligence Corps. However, Berneville-Claye had laughingly responded that he was in the Coldstream Guards and, as a member of the nobility holding only a temporary commission, could not possibly belong to such a corps.

Steiner continues, in his statement, to confirm that Berneville-Claye subsequently moved to Neu-Strelitz, where he remained for about a week or so. Later he learnt from his staff that Berneville-Claye had departed from Neu-Strelitz towards the end of April, in the German Opel staff car that had been provided for his use. In the same timeframe, on 29 April, the day before Hitler committed suicide in his Berlin Führerbunker, Steiner informed his staff officers of his decision to break contact with the Russians, instructing them to order his forces to make their way west and give themselves up to Anglo–American forces.

MacKinnon, the BFC man whom Berneville-Claye had selected as his driver and batman, at the time that he attempted to take the BFC group under command, confirms in his own statement that upon departing Templin they returned to Steiner's headquarters. Here they both stayed for a few days, Berneville-Claye lodging in a nearby house and taking his meals in the German officers' mess, while MacKinnon slept in a caravan and received his food from the soldiers' cookhouse. Later, returning to Templin to find the BFC men already gone, they headed to Neu-Strelitz, having first picked up the landlady and her two daughters from the house in which Berneville-Claye had lodged.[12]

At one stage, they came across and were seen by three other members of the BFC. These renegades were SS-Sturmmanner (Lance

Corporals) Kenneth Berry, Ernest Nicholls and John Somerville, who were walking by the woods near Neu-Strelitz.[13]

Over the next few days, Berneville-Claye and MacKinnon made their way towards the small town of Bad Kleinen, on the north shore of Lake Schwerin, towards which Allied forces were advancing. Stopping overnight in a large mansion full of evacuees, the two of them were awoken the following morning and taken to the local Gestapo headquarters.

However, Berneville-Claye, still in Waffen-SS uniform, smooth-talked his way out of their predicament, and they were released. Continuing their way in the car, they stopped at Gestrow Police Station to get a permit for continued use of the car. At this juncture the vehicle was confiscated from them, although a German officer vouched for Berneville-Claye and so the two were allowed to continue on foot.

Sleeping the night in a farm stable, they were awoken the following morning by a German soldier who told them that the Allies were only about 8 kilometres away. It was 2 May 1945 and, with the American 6th Independent Airborne Brigade almost upon them, Berneville-Claye changed out of and threw away his SS uniform and put on his British uniform. MacKinnon did likewise, but not having a British uniform he instead donned a civilian jacket.

They waited until the American Brigade reached the farm where they had spent the night, and Berneville-Claye then approached and stopped one of the vehicles. He explained that they were British POWs. Therefore, the two of them were allowed to remain with the brigade for the next several days, until the Americans joined up with Russian forces, after which they were passed over to the British.

Within a week, Berneville-Claye was repatriated to England from Germany, on 7 May 1945, the eve of Victory in Europe Day and of Germany signing the surrender.

Chapter 7

British Security Service (MI5) Investigation

In the standard course of events, upon repatriation to England Berneville-Claye was initially sent to Number 15 Officer Reception Unit, Monk Fryston Hall, near Leeds. A month later and while there, on 9 June, he submitted to the commandant, Colonel H.R. Phipps, a report covering his activities in Germany, signing himself off as a captain.[1]

Although Berneville-Claye is generally referred to as a captain during his POW years, he never achieved that rank with the SAS. He was promoted to 'war substantive lieutenant' on 1 October 1942 and, while serving in that rank, was captured some three months later. Upon repatriation to England, on 7 May 1945, his rank remained 'war substantive lieutenant'. When, later, he was cashiered (i.e. dishonourably dismissed) from the Army, on 31 October 1946, his rank was also 'war substantive lieutenant'. Of course, the Germans provided him with the rank of Hauptsturmführer (captain) in the Waffen-SS. Moreover, as we shall see later in this narrative, in August 1945 he briefly worked as a Staff Officer Grade 3 (SO3), in the rank of 'acting captain', with the British War Crimes Executive.

Other British officers who had been POWs in Oflag 79 (which was liberated by American forces on 12 April) and in Stalag XIB were also now in the process of being repatriated to England. Among them was the SBO of Oflag 79, Colonel Brown, who brought with him a copy of the Summary of Evidence. He and a number of other officers volunteered information to the British Security Service. Lieutenant Colonel Vivian Seymer, of MI5, picked up Berneville-Claye's case file. Seymer was already well versed with the BFC, having previously compiled a preliminary report on its activities and those of the radio propaganda units, on 27 March 1945. This report was already being put to good use as the basis for investigations of British renegades.[2]

Upon repatriation to England, many former British POW officers volunteered to rejoin their regiments, or other units destined for service overseas. For although Germany had capitulated, Japan had not, and the war was not yet won in the Far East. Berneville-Claye did not endeavour to do so and, given Stirling's view on him formed during his time in Oflag 79, the SAS certainly would not have welcomed him back into their fold. In any event, with the MI5 investigation pending, this option rapidly closed.

On 3 July, Seymer arranged for a telegram to be dispatched, addressed to Lieutenant Berneville-Claye, 'Chalford', Brownberrie Lane, Horsforth, Leeds (the family home of his second wife, Nina). It instructed him to report for interview with Seymer on 6 July, in Room 55, at the War Office, Whitehall, London. Berneville-Claye duly turned up, but evidently arrived 'wearing captain's pips and a red beret'. He was also spotted as such in Cox & Kings (Lloyds Bank), Pall Mall, with which he had an account.[3]

The red beret referred to was, no doubt, that of the Parachute Regiment (rather than that of the Military Police), and thus neither that of his parent regiment, the West Yorkshire Regiment, nor that of the SAS. Thus, it appears that besides endeavouring to pass himself off as a captain (rather than as a lieutenant), he was also incorrectly dressed in the beret of a regiment to which he did not belong.

Having reported for interview at Room 55 at the War Office, Berneville-Claye was informed by Seymer that certain serious allegations lay against him. He was shown the incriminating buff card with the pencilled notes that had been found amongst his kit at Oflag 79. Berneville-Claye denied having seen the card before. Thereafter, he provided a voluntary statement, under caution, which was conducted by Lieutenant William Savin, of the SIB of the Military Police, with Major G.T.D. Patterson, Intelligence Corps, present throughout. The statement, amounting to five pages of typescript, was conducted over the course of that day and the next.[4]

Berneville-Claye's statement was essentially a more detailed version of the report that he had submitted the previous month, at Monk Fryston, albeit with some notable contradictions. Berneville-Claye explained away his black Waffen-SS uniform by declaring that, having escaped captivity, he had secured it from a refugee family that he had met on the road, and that he had worn it as a disguise while on the run. Thereafter, events, including his arrival at Steiner's headquarters and his meeting there with the BFC men, were, according to him, all part and parcel of a bid to escape. Both his initial report and subsequent statement to MI5 will be considered in more detail later in this narrative, in conjunction with the considered opinion on the case by the office of the Judge Advocate General (JAG).

Three days after Berneville-Claye's interview at the War Office, Patterson dispatched a letter to Mr R.E. Hedger of the Scientific Section, enclosing the buff card, asking him to confirm whether the pencilled words were in Berneville-Claye's handwriting. For comparison purposes, Patterson also enclosed handwritten pencilled notes made by Berneville-Claye during his interview. This was supplemented in the days to come with a further example of his handwriting, in the guise of a letter signed by him.

Following analysis, Hedger responded to Patterson in a detailed letter, on 18 July. He concluded that:

> analysis has revealed a number of definite similarities in letter forms in addition to the general similarity of styles occurring in all three writings. These facts, taken in conjunction with the absence of any marked divergences, in my opinion afford very strong evidence that the writer of the pencilled notes and the letter signed Berneville-Claye also wrote the pencilled words on the card.[5]

Following his initial reception at Monk Fryston, Berneville-Claye was given a period of leave and posted to 6 Infantry Holding Battalion, at Hunstanton, Norfolk. He was there for just a week, from 14 to 21

August, and during that time he was heard boasting that his next posting was to the Control Commission, Germany. Hearing of this, MI5 made it clear to the Army authorities that while under investigation he should not be sent abroad, declaring: 'Berneville-Claye is a notorious liar, and this may only be another flight of his imagination, but we consider that steps should be taken to ensure that he does not leave the country.'[6]

By this stage, MI5 was now considering, prior to the case being referred to the JAG, how best to take it to prosecution, as gathering untainted evidence that was able to stand up in court would be no easy matter. Moreover, MI5 opined: 'Berneville-Claye is a thoroughly nasty bit of work, but he will conduct his defence with a degree of skill.'[7]

However, MI5's letter to the Army authorities arrived too late to stop Berneville-Claye from being posted overseas. Thus, following his week at Hunstanton he was sent, somewhat ironically, to work in the British War Crimes Executive in Germany, as an SO3 in the rank of acting captain. When the paperwork caught up with him, he was dispatched quickly back to England in mid-September. In the interim, the Second World War ended, on 2 September, following the signing by Japan of the surrender document.

Nonetheless, while in Germany for these three weeks Berneville-Claye clearly did very well in his job, as is evident in a letter to the Adjutant General's Branch at the War Office. His commanding officer, Colonel H.J. Phillimore, records that he had remarkable ability, worked extremely hard and efficiently as an administrative officer, and had achieved excellent results in the short period that he had been there.[8]

Berneville-Claye was next posted to a Transport Company, RASC, in Norwich. Here, in October 1945, he commenced an affair with Marie Langley. She was a private soldier in the Auxiliary Territorial Service (ATS), the woman's branch of the Army during the Second World War, and she was serving in his RASC company in Norwich. Marie became pregnant in early November, but when she told him, and later informed Major T. Newlands, their commanding officer, of her condition, Berneville-Claye completely denied the affair. As a result of this and other offences committed while in Norwich, on 21 November 1945 Berneville-Claye was posted away to another RASC company. There he was placed in 'close arrest' for 114 days, pending a trial. Thus, besides the MI5 investigation, he also now had a court martial case hanging over his head.

By mid-December 1945, despite not having interviewed all the witnesses that they wished to, particularly certain German soldiers, MI5 felt compelled to raise Berneville-Claye's case to the attention of the JAG. MI5 had not as yet been able to track down Major Hoffman and Soldat Schmidt from Oflag 79, nor, for that matter, General Steiner. By this time the trials and associated court sentences of other members of the BFC were being publicised in the press. JAG was asked whether there was sufficient evidence to secure a court martial conviction against Berneville-Claye, on charges of collaboration with the enemy while a POW, under Section 4(5) of the Army Act.[9]

The Army Act dealt with military discipline, including certain offences of treachery in relation to the enemy, which were punishable with death. These included: 'having been made a prisoner of war, voluntarily serving with or voluntarily aiding the enemy'; 'treacherously holding correspondence with or giving intelligence to the enemy'; and 'while on active service knowingly doing any act calculated to imperil the success of His Majesty's forces'. It was such offences of treachery, potentially carrying the death penalty, that MI5, the Service authorities, and the JAG were considering and weighing up regarding Berneville-Claye's investigation.

The considered opinion of the JAG was conveyed in a letter from Brigadier H. Shapcott. It outlined that although the evidence thus far gave grounds for the 'very gravest suspicion' against Berneville-Claye, it was not yet strong enough in itself to be certain of securing a conviction of voluntarily aiding the enemy.[10]

Regarding the incriminating buff card found in Berneville-Claye's kit at Oflag 79, Brunswick, although it was almost certainly in his handwriting, there was no direct evidence that he had actually shown it to the Germans, even if he had intended to do so. Moreover, although he was clearly very friendly with the Germans in the camp, and had expressed admiration for them as a people, thus far no concrete evidence had been proffered to demonstrate that he had told them where to search and acted as a stool pigeon. Unless certain Germans, such as Hoffmann, Ackermann or Schmidt, were to testify against him, it was perceived that what had so far been secured in the way of statements from British POWs amounted from an evidential perspective to hearsay.

As regards Berneville-Claye's time at Stalag XIB, Fallingbostel, his initial report and his later statement are clearly contradictory. In his report he states he was incarcerated and interrogated for six days, while in his statement he declares he was only there for three or four days and that nothing unusual happened. While at Fallingbostel, he clearly enjoyed freedom of movement in and out of the camp, particularly in view of his visits to the cinema, on at least one occasion wearing a German captain's uniform. The JAG view was that it was very reasonable to infer from this that he was assisting the Germans in some manner. Nonetheless, there was not sufficient concrete evidence to survive court scrutiny upon which to base a serious charge under Section 4(5) of the Army Act.

Regarding Berneville-Claye's involvement with the BFC, the JAG view was again that the evidence to date amounted only to 'grave suspicion'. Moreover, the evidence of the BFC men, whom Berneville-Claye had encouraged to join him and fight the Russians, would almost certainly be viewed as tainted by the court. Since the BFC men were already in the BFC, the question of them being recruited by Berneville-Claye did not arise.

In addition, although he did indeed exhort them to join him and fight the Russians, this did not occur because they refused to join him. This, as has been related, led to Berneville-Claye's subsequent decision to leave the BFC group, and instead head west with one of the renegades, MacKinnon.

In his report and in his subsequent statement, Berneville-Claye claims that he was given his black SS panzer uniform by a German family, a mother and two daughters, whom he met on the road after he had escaped from a civilian camp near Templin. Nonetheless, this does not explain how he also managed to secure a German field-grey uniform, in which he was first seen when he arrived at Steiner's headquarters.

It appears that Berneville-Claye may have been conflating his claim of having been given his black SS panzer uniform by a 'mother and two daughters' near Templin with the occasion when he lodged with a 'landlady and two daughters', near Templin. If in his story he had in mind the same mother and two daughters, then his claim was flawed, for he lodged with the landlady and two daughters after he had left Steiner's headquarters. By this stage he had already been seen, by several witnesses, in both his German field-grey uniform and his black SS uniform.

Berneville-Claye claims in his report that he 'played the part of a rat to the full' in front of the BFC men he met there, as part of an escape plan. Regardless, even if the BFC renegades did testify against him, their evidence was likely to be viewed as tainted, while his defence was based on a story that he was only 'playing a part' in a bid to escape.

Thereafter, Berneville-Claye's report and statement prove contradictory once again. In the report he states he received a posting from Steiner's headquarters to an Armoured Car Unit of the Nordland Division, while in the statement he declares he was informed that he was being sent to the SS Propaganda Department. Regardless, at this stage, with the war lost by Germany, he managed to secure a car and, with the Allies advancing from the west, now headed in their direction. However improbable and contradictory Berneville-Claye's tale – and he himself declared it to be 'an incredible story' – JAG perceived that it would be difficult to disprove in court, given the evidence available.

The JAG view was that even if he had been a BFC member, there was no firm evidence that he had ever worked for the BFC. Moreover, it was open to some doubt whether mere membership of the BFC was sufficient to justify such a serious charge – punishable with death – under Section 4(5) of the Army Act.

Early the following year, in February 1946, with General Steiner a prisoner of war, held now at Island Camp, Bridgend, Glamorgan, he was brought to the London District Cage. He was interrogated on what he knew of the BFC, and more specifically of Berneville-Claye. The search was still on for Hoffman and Schmidt. MI5 perceived this task as analogous to looking for needles in a haystack, given that both Germans had such common names.

The camp commandant at Oflag 79, Oberst (Colonel) Strehle, and his successor, Oberst Otto Sauer, who had taken over on 25 January 1945, were also both being sought, as was Ackermann, the SS political officer who acted also as the camp commandant's specialist interpreter, and Stock, another specialist interpreter at the camp.

Steiner was duly interrogated in London and provided a lengthy statement, but he offered nothing that unduly incriminated Berneville-Claye. Given Steiner's Waffen-SS status, it is perhaps understandable that he did not wish to condemn the BFC men, nor 'the English Officer', as Berneville-Claye is referred to, as he was unwilling or unable to recall him by name, for such men had ostensibly volunteered to fight for the same cause as he had. Steiner himself was under investigation for war crimes and in due course faced charges at the Nuremberg Trials, although these were subsequently dropped for lack of solid evidence, and he was released.

In correspondence, in February 1946, between Colonel W.A. Hinchley-Cooke of MI5 and Brigadier H. Shapcott of JAG, and which took account of Berneville-Claye's own statement, there was agreement between them that the English officer of whom Steiner spoke was undoubtedly Berneville-Claye. However, from a legal perspective his 'conduct whilst with Steiner was considered equally consistent with innocence as with guilt.' It was clear that stronger evidence would need to be secured from elsewhere.[11] Sauer's subsequent interrogation, in early April, also offered nothing of significant value.

Meanwhile, with the MI5 treachery investigation ongoing, Berneville-Claye was called to stand trial on account of his conduct while posted with the RASC transport company at Norwich. This was the first court martial of two for which he stood trial in 1946, and it was held at Fenham Barracks, Newcastle, on 3 April.[12] On this occasion he was charged with a total of thirteen offences of the Army Act, specifically: eight charges under section 40, three charges under Section 16, one charge under Section 18(4), and one charge under Section 15(1). These charges related to cheques issued without adequate funds, stealing public petrol, using an official vehicle without permission, going absent without leave (AWOL), besides improper association with a private soldier, Marie Langley, ATS.

Between Marie's affair with Berneville-Claye, in October 1945, and his court martial in April 1946, she became married to an ex-member of the US Air Force, and so appeared at court under her new surname, Hanf. When she was called to give witness and was asked 'Are you going to have the accused's child?' she answered, 'Yes. My husband is aware of the situation. I told him everything.'[13]

Marie, aged 20, explained to the court that when she told Berneville-Claye, then aged 28, that she was pregnant, he had informed her that if she kept quiet then he would help her. But if the matter became public knowledge, he'd deny all responsibility. Moreover, he went on to declare that his father was an earl, who'd take the matter to court to defend him, for if the scandal came out it might ruin his chances. In this threat there were echoes of his earlier threats, in his letter to Ada Metcalfe, a decade previously.

Berneville-Claye was duly sentenced by court martial to be cashiered. However, his luck held again on this occasion, for this sentence was afterwards adjusted by the GOC 'to be severely reprimanded and to lose a year's seniority'.

Subsequently, Marie gave birth to a boy at Coventry Municipal Hospital, on 4 August 1946, although he was given no name at birth. The baby's birth certificate does not state his father's name, but records that he was put up for adoption.[14] This baby was Berneville-Claye's fourth (and second illegitimate) child that he had thus far sired, none of whom he had endeavoured to take any responsibility for.

The court martial, and his affair with Marie (née Langley), was reported by the *News of the World* newspaper, on 7 April 1946, under the headline 'Ex ATS Girl Says She Visited Billet'. This was how Berneville-Claye's first wife, Irene (née Palmer), married to him in October 1936, first heard of his whereabouts after he had abandoned her and their daughter, Yvonne, some ten years previously. Moreover, the news report highlighted that Berneville-Claye was married, with a 5-year old son. This was how Irene also learnt that he had subsequently married bigamously a second wife, Nina (née Payne), in March 1940, with whom he had a son, Graeme.

Consequently, Berneville-Claye was subsequently charged at Otley, Yorkshire, with bigamy, and was committed for trial at Leeds Assizes. The prosecuting solicitor read to the magistrates what he described as 'a remarkable statement' attributed to Berneville-Claye, who alleged 'that a girl [i.e. Irene (née Palmer)] was the prime mover in his marriage at the age of 17'. Accordingly, the following day the *News of The World* report ran with the headline 'Girl Prime Mover In My Wedding at 17'.[15] Berneville-Claye was in fact 18, just a month shy of 19, when he married Irene in 1936. Irene, by this time living in Surbiton (and later to die of stomach cancer in 1960), chose not to make a statement at the bigamy trial, although her brother-in-law, Alan Hayes, gave evidence that he had been a witness at her 1936 wedding.

Nina (née Payne), by this stage living in Great Ouseburn, York (and later to die in 1999), confirmed at the bigamy trial that while her husband, Berneville-Claye, had been in the forces she had drawn allowances as his wife. However, Berneville-Claye's luck again held. He did not go to prison, but instead was sentenced, on 4 July 1946, only to be bound over for twelve months and required not to reoffend.[16]

Following Berneville-Claye's first court martial of 1946, he was posted away and served in several different locations, and it appears that the Army had difficulty in finding a role for him. During this period, with the MI5 investigation still in train, he nonetheless managed to fall foul of the military authorities once again. This resulted in his second court martial that same year.

Berneville-Claye's second court martial of 1946 commenced on 17 September. On this occasion he was found guilty on four charges – specifically, two of stealing a quantity of coal and petrol, one of improperly using a War Department vehicle, and one for stealing a typewriter. He was sentenced to be cashiered and to be imprisoned for six months. As later officially recorded in the *London Gazette*, on 7 January 1947: 'War Substantive Lieutenant D.W. St. A. Berneville-Claye (207721) is cashiered by sentence of a general court martial, on 31 October 1946.'

Seth suggests that at Berneville-Claye's second court martial of 1946, it was also taken into account that he had illicitly extracted fifty pounds from a Scotsman. This was achieved by offering to provide legal advice, while posing in the guise of Captain the Honourable Berneville-Claye, DSO, MC, an adjutant in the Coldstream Guards, attached to the Judge Advocate's Office. Moreover, Wikipedia suggests that at his first 1946 court martial he had also been charged with wearing the ribbon of the DSO. The Australian newspaper *Campbelltown Macarthur Advertiser* later reported that he was court-martialled and demoted for wearing the ribbon of the DSO, which he claimed he had been awarded. Whatever the veracity of this matter, there appears to be a degree of conflation in these various reports.

Regarding Berneville-Claye's right to wear medals, many years later the British Army Medals Office confirmed that due to the nature of his conduct and having been cashiered from the Army, he had forfeited all entitlement to medals. Under other circumstances, he may have been entitled to wear four Second World War medals, these being the 1939–45 Star, the Africa Star (with 8th Army clasp), the Defence Medal (1939–45), and the War Medal (1939–45).

However, regardless of his forfeiture to such medals, this did not stop him, later in civilian life, from wearing a row of nine miniature medals with evening dress. These included the Military Cross and French Croix de Guerre (both for gallantry), which he evidently saw fit to award to himself. Legislation making the unauthorised wearing of official medals a criminal offence was originally introduced in the aftermath of the First World War by the then Secretary for War, Winston Churchill. But evidently this did not deter Berneville-Claye from sporting them.

Throughout the latter part of 1946, MI5 and the Army continued their quest for the German military witnesses that might possibly provide firm evidence to stand up in court. However, increasingly they were drawing blanks, and statements that may have incriminated Berneville-Claye were likely also to incriminate the Germans providing it, for some, such as Steiner and Berger, were themselves also being tried for war crimes. Having finally caught up with Stock, from Oflag 79, he informed them that the Schmidt that they had been seeking for the last several months was actually 'Schmitz'. Thus, they had been on a wild goose chase. Hoffman, the Abwehr security officer, was tracked down, but he proved unhelpful, and it seemed that Ackermann, the SS political officer, had evaded the Allies and slipped over the border into Switzerland.

Throughout, Berneville-Claye stuck doggedly to his story, strongly denying any involvement as a POW informant, or as a Waffen-SS officer and BFC member, other than as a ruse in an endeavour to escape. By March 1947, MI5 concluded that a trial for treachery, under Section 4(5) of the Army Act, was unlikely to succeed. From an evidential perspective, nothing significant had been unearthed since the previous December, when JAG had advised that there was still insufficient concrete evidence. JAG's view was that although Berneville-Claye's story was wildly improbable, his behaviour was extremely questionable, and though it was believed he had lied recklessly, the necessary solid evidence that might stand up in court and prove that he was guilty of treachery had not been secured.[17]

Meanwhile, in 1945, three British renegades, William Joyce, John Amery and Theodore Schurch, had gone on trial for their lives and been hanged. Joyce was committed for trial at the Central Criminal Court (the 'Old Bailey') in September 1945 and charged with three counts of high treason. He did not deny his actions, but he denied the actions amounted to treason. Nonetheless, he was judged guilty. Subsequently, on 3 January 1946, he was executed by the hangman, Albert Pierrepoint, at Wandsworth Prison. As such, Joyce was the last person to be executed in Britain for treason.

John Amery's trial was an altogether quicker affair. His trial lasted just eight minutes. For when he went to the Old Bailey, in November 1945, he immediately pleaded guilty to eight charges of high treason. These included recruiting British POWs into the BFC and making pro-Nazi propaganda broadcasts for Germany. He was sentenced to death and executed by Pierrepoint, on 19 December 1945. Pierrepoint described Amery as 'the bravest person I'd ever hanged'. When he was led to the Wandsworth Prison scaffold by his executioner, Amery nonchalantly quipped, 'I've always wanted to meet you, Mr Pierrepoint, though not of course under these circumstances!'

Theodore Schurch, the RASC soldier who had specialised in eliciting information from captured SAS and LRDG men, was charged under the Treachery Act 1940, rather than for treason. Working as a spy and stool pigeon for both Italian and German military intelligence, he had proved to be extremely effective. Even the captured David Stirling, while being held in Rome, inadvertently disclosed to Schurch that his successor as CO of the SAS was Paddy Mayne.[18] Tried by court martial at the Duke of York's Headquarters, Chelsea, in September 1945, Schurch was found guilty on nine counts of treachery and one of desertion with intent to join the enemy. The only British soldier executed for treachery committed during the Second World War, Schurch was hanged at Pentonville Prison, on 4 January 1946 (one day after Joyce). He was the last person to be executed in the UK for treachery, and the last to be executed for any offence other than murder.

Thomas Cooper, who had early in the war joined the Waffen-SS and latterly joined and become a BFC mainstay, was put on trial for high treason. As was Roy Walter Purdy, Royal Navy Reserve, who played a significant part working for the German Büro Concordia black propaganda radio station. Cooper was tried at the Old Bailey, London, in January 1946. In his defence he maintained the fiction that, in a desire to serve Britain, he had joined the BFC as a means of securing military intelligence for the British. But he was found guilty and sentenced to hang. However, he was reprieved, and his sentence was commuted to life imprisonment, on the basis that he had been a follower in treason rather than a leader and recruiter. Purdy was also sentenced to hang, but similarly to Cooper and for the same reasons, his sentence was also commuted to life imprisonment. Both these men were released from prison within ten years.

The lesser renegades also had their day in court, although imprisonment, rather than death by hanging, tended to be the sentences for their treachery. Given that MI5 already had a clear understanding of who they were, the majority were arrested with comparative ease in May 1945 or shortly thereafter. Moreover, MI5 had also previously formed a specialist task force to deal with their arrests and subsequent interrogation, which proved to be extremely effective.

This task force included detectives seconded to MI5 from Scotland Yard and commissioned into the Intelligence Corps. Foremost amongst them were Leonard Burt, William Skardon and Reginald Spooner. During their investigations the detectives were subjected to a similar litany of lame excuses from the BFC renegades as to why they had sided with Germany. Foremost among these excuses were that they had joined the BFC to escape from their POW camps (as was Berneville-Claye's claim), or as a means of sabotaging the BFC, or to gather intelligence and spy on the other BFC renegades. No serious credence was given to these fictions, nor sympathy provided to those Britons who had chosen to side with the enemy and don the uniform of the Waffen-SS.

The court sentences meted out to these British lesser renegades tended to range from between ten to fifteen years' imprisonment, although some sentences were later reduced. Regarding the Commonwealth renegades, there was a good deal more disparity in their court sentences – dependent, seemingly, on how Canada, South

Africa, New Zealand and Australia viewed their crimes of treason and treachery against the British Crown.

Pleasants escaped a British jail term altogether, for the British authorities considered that he had suffered enough already. When the Russians had encircled Berlin, Pleasants donned a Wehrmacht uniform, in lieu of his BFC one, and he and his recently wedded German SS wife escaped, taking to the sewers. While doing so, and when set upon by two German soldiers, they were compelled to kill them both in the ensuing struggle. Under an assumed German identity and working as an interpreter, Pleasants managed to eke out a living. However, the following year he and his wife were arrested by the Soviets on suspicion of spying. Pleasants was sent to the Vorkuta Gulag forced-labour camp, in the Russian Arctic, where he was incarcerated for several years. Pleasants was eventually repatriated to England, in 1952, but was never able to locate his German wife.

Grave suspicion of Berneville-Claye's guilt persisted in the minds of many in MI5 and the military authorities. However, it was recognised that BFC witness testimonies were likely to be viewed as tainted, and insufficient unimpeachable evidence had been secured to take him to court for treachery. Thus, against the backdrop that he had twice in 1946 been found guilty at courts martial, and on the second occasion had been cashiered and imprisoned for six months, the treachery investigation was dropped in March 1947. Therefore, while Berneville-Clay was still in prison, his MI5 file was closed.

Chapter 8

Civvy Street

Having been cashiered from the Army the previous autumn and served six months in prison following his court martial, Berneville-Claye was released in the spring of 1947. In the interim, the MI5 treachery investigation had been dropped and the file closed. He now had the opportunity of a relatively fresh start and of finding his way in civilian life.

However, Seth maintains that Berneville-Claye was subsequently in and out of the civilian courts, over the next few years, on a variety of charges, finally disappearing from view when the Recorder of London sentenced him to a year in prison on finding him guilty of fraudulent conversion. Seth does not elaborate upon the specifics of the offence, where Berneville-Claye was tried and sentenced for fraudulent conversion, or whether he actually went to prison. However, as we shall see later, in 1967, UK police at New Scotland Yard confirmed that this was indeed the case, in communication with the Australian Police concerning a subsequent offence in the Australian capital, Canberra.

Following his military service, Berneville-Claye's activities do indeed become harder to track, but he does not disappear from view. Although he slipped off to Australia in 1959, one is still able to establish a fair amount of further detail concerning his movements and activities, both before and after 1972, the publication date of Seth's book.

It appears that Berneville-Claye was in Paris between February and August 1949. This came to light early the following year when he gave evidence in January 1950, on the sixth day of the infamous trial of Brian Donald Hume who had murdered a car dealer, Stanley Setty, in the autumn of 1949. The facts of the murder case are gruesome, and Berneville-Claye's involvement, as a witness, bizarre to say the least.

Setty, a second-hand car dealer and petty criminal, was last seen alive on 4 October 1949. One of his business partners in crime was Hume, ex-Royal Air Force, criminal and conman. A heated argument and struggle broke out between the two men while in Hume's flat in Finchley Road, London, as a result of Setty having earlier that day kicked Hume's dog. Jealousy was also reasonably likely to have been a contributing factor, for it may have been that Setty was perceived by Hume as taking an undue interest in his wife.

Having killed Setty with a German SS dagger during the struggle, Hume then devised a means of disposing of the body. He came up with the plan of dismembering the corpse and then dropping the body parts over the English Channel by light plane. He hid the body in the coal cupboard that first night. Then, over the next two days, despite the comings and goings of both his wife and a cleaning lady, Hume nonetheless contrived to clean up the evidence of the bloody struggle and remove Setty's body from his flat.

Using a linoleum knife to cut to the bone and then a hacksaw, he dismembered Setty's body, which he wrapped up in three parcels and smuggled out of the flat. The day following the murder, on 5 October, he took the first two parcels, one containing Setty's head and the other containing his two legs, and drove to the United Services Flying Club at Elstree Aerodrome. Having arranged to hire an Auster light plane (registration G-AGXT), as an aerodrome club member, he loaded his two parcels, suitably weighted, and filed a flight plan to Southend. Once airborne, he diverted to the English Channel and, with the coastline of France in sight, dropped the two parcels, along with the SS dagger, linoleum knife and hacksaw, out of the plane. Hume then circled overhead and watched while the two parcels sank beneath the waves, before, with daylight now fading, landing at Southend Airfield, rather than at Elstree.

The following day, on 6 October, Hume first collected his car from Elstree. Then, with the unwitting assistance of a decorator whom he had arranged to help clean up his flat, he carried the third and much heavier parcel containing Setty's torso and arms down to his car. He then drove to Southend Airfield, where he found the Auster already refuelled and ready for him. He drove his car close to the plane and loaded the heavy package into the passenger seat of the light-blue aircraft, and then took off.

However, having flown out over the English Channel, Hume then had great difficulty in heaving the package out of the plane while maintaining control of the aircraft. In the process of disposing of the package, the blanket and lead weights in which the torso was wrapped became loose. Moreover, when Hume looked down, he saw to his consternation that the torso was floating on the surface of the sea. There was nothing for it but to head back for land. But he never reached Elstree. In failing light and running low on fuel, he made it only as far as Gravesend Airport, having first landed in a field near Faversham and checked with a farmer upon his bearings. The following day, 7 October, Hume tidied up the loose ends, collected his car from Southend and arranged for the Auster to be returned to Elstree Aerodrome from Gravesend.

Within a fortnight, Setty's torso was washed up on the Essex mudflats at Dengie Flats and, on 21 October, was discovered by a wildfowler who was out hunting. The police were able to identify the torso from the fingerprints, these being known to the police, given that Setty had served time in prison. It was not long before the trail led the police to Hume, who was duly arrested, on 27 October, and taken to Albany Street Police Station for questioning. The following day he was moved to Bow Street Police Station and there charged with the murder of Setty. Then, on 29 October, Hume appeared in court at Bow Street and, following a three-minute hearing, was remanded in custody at Brixton Prison. He appeared again before magistrates at Bow Street on 16 November, during which time evidence from twenty-three witnesses was heard, and Hume's trial was fixed for mid-January 1950.

At his Old Bailey trial, which commenced on 18 January 1950, Hume denied murder but admitted dropping the three parcels over the English Channel. The hangman's rope awaited him, if found guilty of murder, for capital punishment was still extant in Britain. Hume concocted an elaborate story about how he had been offered cash by three gangsters. These men, known to him only as 'Mac' (or 'Max'), 'Greeny' (or 'Green'), and 'The Boy', had allegedly asked him to hide the three packages in his flat and then drop them over the sea by light aircraft. During his trial Hume did not deny wrongdoing, but he maintained that he was not guilty of the murder itself.

On 25 January, the sixth day of the trial, Hume's defence team produced a surprise witness, who declared that the previous year he had become involved with a criminal gang in Paris. His testimony, including descriptions and gang names, helped corroborate Hume's story. This served to cast doubt in the minds of the jury, who were left wondering whether the gang did in fact exist and, if so, whether Hume had perhaps only been an unwitting accomplice. This surprise witness was none other than Berneville-Claye, who was described as 'a youngish, fair-haired man with an intelligent face and an educated voice'.[1]

Hume's defence team introduced their final witness as follows: 'Mr Douglas Clay, a writer, of Gloucester Avenue, North-West London; this witness was not available to us until late last night and came to us through channels we knew nothing about.' When questioned by the defence team, Berneville-Claye declared that he had travelled to Paris on 23 February the previous year, 1949, and remained there for some six months, until August. He confirmed that while in Paris he had met several gang members who were engaged in smuggling arms to Palestine and cars to Britain. He then went on to describe to the jury that two of the gang's 'strong-arm' members were known as 'Maxie' and 'The Boy',[2] thus, strikingly similar names to those of the criminals, 'Max' and 'The Boy', whom Hume had identified.

Berneville-Claye described himself to the court as a freelance journalist and scriptwriter. During cross-examination by the Crown prosecutor, he declared that he had come to know the gang while endeavouring to cash some traveller's cheques with a man he had met at a Paris nightclub. When he had accompanied this nightclub acquaintance back to his hotel room to conduct the cash transaction, the man had been arrested by the police. Because Berneville-Claye had been present at the time of the man's arrest, this incident had apparently then given him kudos and an entrée to the criminal gang.

The court was encouraged to believe that the recent publicity of the Hume trial had reminded Berneville-Claye of these events, and that he had come forward to offer his testimony as a civic-minded citizen. Moreover, he declared that he had never seen Hume in his life. When asked what he had done with this information, Berneville-Claye said that he had reported it to the French Sûreté Nationale, to the British Embassy in Paris, to Scotland Yard, and thereafter had contacted Hume's defence team. In summing up to the jury, Hume's defence team referred to Berneville-Claye's testimony, concerning the gang members' names. The question was posed to them, 'In the light of that sort of evidence, can you for a moment accept the fact that all three men never existed and are a product of the fertile imagination of Mr Hume?'[3]

If Berneville-Claye's evidence had been intended to sow seeds of doubt in the minds of the jury, it certainly worked. Indeed, on 26 January, the final day of the trial, the jury were unable to agree on the murder charge and therefore the judge was compelled to discharge the hung jury. Immediately, a second jury was sworn in and instructed by the judge to return a verdict of 'not guilty' on the murder charge, but to consider a second indictment on Hume's file – that of him being an 'accessory after the fact to murder': knowing that a certain person or person unknown, on 4 October 1949, murdered Setty, and that on 5 or 6 October he assisted by disposing of Setty's body.

When asked by the judge whether he pleaded guilty or not guilty to this second indictment, Hume quickly pleaded guilty. He was sentenced by the judge to twelve years' imprisonment. However, he served eight years only, having earned maximum remission for good behaviour, and was released from Dartmoor Prison on 1 February 1958.

Upon his release from prison, and finding himself short of money, Hume decided to sell his murder confession and full account to a newspaper, the *Sunday Pictorial* (now the *Sunday Mirror*). He received £2,000 for his story, which was published by the paper in June 1958. Under the 'double jeopardy' legal safeguard, Hume knew that he could not be tried for the same crime twice. Moreover, he calculated that if he were subsequently tried for perjury, he could declare that the newspaper story was a lie committed for money, and reaffirm the testimony given at his original trial.

Hume confessed to the murder in full, and he also confirmed that his story of the three members of the gang, 'Max', 'Greeny' and 'The Boy', was a complete fabrication. He also said that he had based his descriptions of the three members of the gang upon the three policemen who had arrested him for the murder. This revelation, in turn, raised further serious questions, particularly concerning the motive and truth of Berneville-Claye's own testimony, for his evidence regarding 'Maxie' and 'The Boy', which Hume's defence team had used eight years previously at the end of the trial to sow seeds of doubt, had resulted in a hung jury.

Despite the double jeopardy legal safeguard, Hume nonetheless decided he was unsafe in England and, adopting a false identity, moved to Switzerland in late May 1958, just prior to the publication of his story. He continued his life of crime, robbing banks at gunpoint. Eventually, in a bungled armed robbery on a Zurich bank in January 1959, during which he shot and killed a man, he was captured. Charged with murder at his trial in September 1959, Hume was found guilty and sentenced to life imprisonment with hard labour. In 1976 he was judged to be insane and transferred from Regensdorf Prison in Switzerland to the Broadmoor Institution for the criminally insane, in England.

But why, in 1950, did Berneville-Claye go to the trouble of volunteering to give evidence for Hume, whom, he declared in court, he had never seen in his life? Had Berneville-Claye really become a civic-minded citizen? This, despite declaring in court that he had recently been in Paris, mixing with a criminal gang of smugglers, and that they had accepted him within their circle. None of this had cast him in a favourable light, particularly in a venue such as the Old Bailey, surrounded by court officials, police and reporters.

Was it perhaps the case that Berneville-Claye did in fact know Hume, and that he felt he owed him some kind of favour? The two men had several experiences in common. Both had joined and undergone RAF basic training in a similar timeframe. Berneville-Claye had joined the RAF on 8 September 1939, as an aircrew trainee at Cardington, and had subsequently conducted his aircrew training at Cambridge, until he was discharged on 27 March 1940. Hume had joined on 7 September 1939 and conducted his basic training at Uxbridge and Debden, and subsequently at Hastings. He became very unwell in early 1940, and eventually was medically discharged on 13 May 1941. Thus, they had joined the RAF within a day of one another and, although at different RAF bases, perhaps they had first met at some stage during their basic training.

After his short period of RAF service, Berneville-Claye had ended up in court, in 1940, for posing as an RAF officer and stealing cheques. Hume adopted a similar modus operandi after he left the RAF in 1941, although he managed to get away with it for far longer. Dressed as an RAF officer and with a false identity card, in the guise of 'Flying Officer Donald Hume', he essentially worked as a conman, passing dud cheques, until his arrest in April 1942. He was charged and appeared at the Old Bailey, on 24 June, but got off lightly, only being bound over for two years and fined five pounds.

Although neither of the two men secured a pilot's licence while in the RAF, Hume later took up flying lessons. He obtained his Royal Aero Club aviator certificate in March 1949, from Elstree Aerodrome, and this civilian 'C' pilot's licence qualified him to fly solo. Hume confessed, later in 1950, that he took up smuggling and was known in his circles as 'the flying smuggler', trading in all forms of illegal commodities, including firearms. This smuggling racket was of course relatively short-lived, from April to September 1949 only, and Hume also admitted to having criminal contacts in Paris.

During this period Berneville-Claye was also in Paris, from February to August 1949, rubbing shoulders with a gang of smugglers who traded in illegal firearms and stolen cars. If not before, then this might have been when and how the two men met. This then may well explain why Berneville-Claye felt compelled to appear as a witness at Hume's trial in January 1950, in support of him, sowing seeds of doubt with the jury.

Hume was known to often embellish his stories, particularly concerning his prowess behind the controls of planes and fast cars, and so one must be prepared to take some of what he said with a pinch of salt. He was particularly obsessed with planes and flight, and often told tall tales about his heroic escapades during the war with the RAF, no doubt as counterweight to the fact that his RAF record had actually been extremely mundane.

Therefore, one can't but wonder whether Hume was familiar with James Thurber's short story *The Secret Life of Walter Mitty*, published in 1939, of which a film was made in 1947. The subject of the book concerns a very ordinary young man who daydreams and fantasises about being a hero, including a heroic RAF pilot in the war. Of course, Berneville-Claye was also not averse to embellishing the facts and telling tall tales. Thus, if they ever met, over a beer or two, no doubt some extraordinary stories were shared between the two fantasists.

Having returned to London from Paris in August 1949, Berneville-Claye had met and married, in September, Margaret Jean Murdoch (1925–94), at Tipton, near Wednesbury, Staffordshire. Nine months after having met, they had a son, Guy, born on 23 May 1950, his fifth child. This transpired to be Berneville-Claye's second bigamous marriage, and in the event did not last long. He and his new family lived for a while on a Suffolk farm. Guy, who later had a son and daughter of his own, relates that while living on the farm, Berneville-Claye was caught, in flagrante delicto, having sex with a farm girl. Whether there was ever a child resulting from this affair is unknown.

Not surprisingly, Berneville-Claye's affair with the farm girl did not go down well with Margaret, who was even less amused when it came to light that he had married her bigamously. When it became known that Berneville-Claye was still married to Irene, he was brought to court. It will be recalled that at his trial in 1946, for his bigamous marriage to Nina, he was sentenced only to be bound over for twelve months and required not to reoffend. However, offend for a second time he did. Thus, when Berneville-Claye was taken to court for his bigamous marriage to Margaret (who later took the name Mitchell), he was sentenced to serve a custodial sentence at Pentonville Prison, London. One may presume that, as a result, his legitimate marriage to Irene was subsequently dissolved, for in 1953 he married again.

After Berneville-Claye had served his sentence in Pentonville Prison for bigamy and been released, he shortly thereafter met Gisela, a German-born lady, at a party while she was in UK visiting her cousin. (The pseudonym 'Greta' is used in Metcalfe's book.) At around this stage, in 1950 to 1951, Berneville-Claye apparently also suffered some form of nervous breakdown, perhaps reactive depression, following his prison release, quite possibly because of the extensive amount of time he had spent in custody, in one form or another, including time spent as a prisoner of war.

Berneville-Claye married Gisela in Watford, Hertfordshire, in December 1953. This was his fourth marriage, and their marriage certificate records his name as 'Claye, Douglas, W.B.' and gives his occupation as a farmer. By this stage Gisela had given birth to their first child, Andrew, later a policeman and lawyer (who in due course married Sharon). Moreover, Gisela was also pregnant with their second son, Colin (who later had a son of his own, Liam). A couple of years later, Berneville-Claye and Gisela had a third son, Peter, and three years thereafter a daughter, Susan (who later emigrated to South Africa and moved to a small town in the Western Cape).

At this stage, in 1953, some sixteen years after he had left Irene, his first wife, Berneville-Claye also contrived to track her down using a private detective. However, before meeting her, he first paid a visit to the baker's shop in which he had discovered that their 16-year-old daughter, Yvonne, was working. Early one evening, while she was shutting up shop, she saw a man looking at her through the shop window, who then introduced himself as her father. Berneville-Claye asked her to accompany him, as he wanted to visit Irene. Yvonne declined to get on the back of his motorbike and instead made her own way home, and told her mother whom she had just met, out of the blue. Berneville-Claye arrived at the house shortly thereafter, and Yvonne recalls that when her mother opened the front door and saw Berneville-Claye, she visibly aged ten years.

Nonetheless, Berneville-Claye asked Yvonne to come and live with him and his new family. It appeared that he might wish to make amends, but understandably, Yvonne and Irene were both extremely wary of him; after all, where had he been for the past sixteen years? Yvonne declined to move in with Berneville-Claye and his new family, although she did visit him on a few weekends.

At this time, Berneville-Claye was of course with Gisela, his fourth wife. He happened to be living in some style, in a large manor-style house in the village of Chipperfield, Hertfordshire, some 5 miles north of Watford, where they had married, and was riding to hounds. The local hunt, the Old Berkeley, often met on the lawns in front of their house, and Yvonne recalls that Berneville-Claye played the squire, on horseback, resplendent in hunting pink. He also became very actively involved in a local theatre group, and this is perhaps why he sometimes described himself as a playwright. Yvonne also recalls that Andrew, his first son with Gisela, was still a small baby, and she was at the time pregnant with their second son, Colin.

One example of Berneville-Claye's theatre work was George Landen Dann's play *Caroline Chisholm*, in which he played the character Styles. The play documents Caroline Chisholm, one of the great figures in nineteenth-century Australian history, and her work in helping young immigrant women arriving in Australia in the early colonial era. Aired by the Australian Broadcasting Corporation a couple of years later, little did Berneville-Claye know it at the time but in a few years, he himself would depart for Australia.[4]

The following year, 1954, Yvonne and her future husband, Lydell Newby, US Air Force, had to secure a court ruling to overturn Berneville-Claye's refusal of consent to their marriage. In those days one needed parental consent to marry if one had not yet reached the age of 21. Berneville-Claye never turned up at court to explain his reasons, which, the family believed, were not on account of Yvonne's young age, but simply that she had refused to comply with his wishes for her to move into his house. In this episode there is a glimpse of the domineering and controlling side of Berneville-Claye's personality.

In Berneville-Claye's absence, the magistrate ruled against him. Yvonne and Lydell were married in Surbiton, Surrey, that summer of 1954, and on their marriage certificate Berneville-Claye is described as a playwright. Yvonne and her husband subsequently moved to Wisconsin, America, and although they later divorced, they remained on good terms. Yvonne never saw Berneville-Claye or Gisela again.

There is a photograph of Berneville-Claye in this period, mid-1950s, at a New Year's Eve party, standing next to his elder brother, Derek, with his wife, Gisela, and his mother, Daisy, sitting in front of them. Berneville-Claye is dressed resplendent in 'white tie' and black dress coat with tails. Upon his chest he is wearing a row of nine miniature medals, including the Military Cross and French Croix de Guerre (both for gallantry) that he had evidently seen fit to award himself.[5]

In the late 1950s, Berneville-Claye moved with Gisela and their three young sons to Ilkley town, Yorkshire. Here the family moved into Yewbank House, and it was here that their daughter, Susan, was born in August 1958. Meanwhile, Berneville-Claye secured employment in nearby Leeds as a salesman with Rank Xerox. All seemed very well set for him and his new family.

However, it was also in Ilkley town that Berneville-Claye commenced an affair, in 1957, with a neighbour's wife, 'Jenny' (a pseudonym used by Metcalfe), a married woman who also had children of her own. As a result of their affair, she became pregnant and then panicked, so Berneville-Claye and Jenny eloped together to the Mediterranean.

Meanwhile, Gisela and her young family were left stranded in Ilkley, with no idea as to whether Berneville-Claye might ever return. Neighbours helped Gisela as best they could, but things were not easy, for Berneville-Claye had borrowed money from several people in town without repaying it, and the debt-recovery men were also looking to reclaim furniture and other household items of value from their house.

However, after Jenny's money had run out in the Mediterranean, Berneville-Claye returned to his wife, Gisela, in England, leaving Jenny abroad with no funds, and endeavoured to spin a tale that she had led him astray. Because of this affair, Jenny and her husband felt compelled to move away from Ilkley, were later divorced, and she had a baby boy who was put up for adoption. This was Berneville-Claye's tenth child, only four of whom (those born to Gisela) he did not abandon along with their mothers.

Although Jenny soon enough came to realise Berneville-Claye's fundamentally selfish side, she remembers Gisela with affection. Moreover, she recalls a car accident in which Gisela's face was badly scarred. Berneville-Claye had been driving, while drunk, when he had crashed the car. It had subsequently taken several operations involving plastic surgery to repair the damage to Gisela's face, but fortunately the surgeons were able to work wonders.

Following the scandal with Jenny, Berneville-Claye was forced, in February 1958, to leave Rank Xerox, and he was replaced at the company. This was a heavy blow, for the job would likely have proved extremely profitable, providing much-needed financial security. Nonetheless, Berneville-Claye and his family stayed on in Ilkley for a while.

When Berneville-Claye eventually departed Ilkley, he owed money all over town. Between November 1958 and December 1981, he was served some ten Bankruptcy Act notices. Published in the *London Gazette* (Supplement), these notices detail the efforts, in this regard, of Harrogate Court and the Official Receiver's Office, Leeds.[6] However, by this stage Berneville-Claye had long departed England's shores.

Chapter 9

Australia

Berneville-Claye evidently felt compelled to make a clean break of things, and so decided to emigrate with his family from England to Australia. Aboard the SS *Strathnaver* and bound for Melbourne, they docked on 14 March 1959 at the port city of Fremantle, on the Swan River, near Perth, Western Australia.[1] Having set sail the previous month, on 15 February, from London's Tilbury Docks, on the river Thames, their passage had taken them via the Suez Canal and Bombay.

The SS *Strathnaver* was a handsome ship and had been the first P&O passenger liner to adopt the white hull and buff funnels that later became the P&O signature livery. During the war she had been requisitioned for service as a troopship, to transport Australian and New Zealand forces to the Middle East. By the time Berneville-Claye and his family sailed in her, she had been converted to a one-class ship with berths for 1,252 passengers. In view of the subsequent decision by the Australian Government to cancel forward bookings for supported-passage British emigrants, her last voyage to Australia was in 1961. As a result, P&O announced her withdrawal, sold her for scrap, and her final voyage was from London to Hong Kong in the spring of 1962.

By 1963, Berneville–Claye and his family were living in Thornbury, in the electoral Division of Batman in the northern suburbs of Melbourne, Victoria. It may be that it was here, at some stage, that he first worked as a radio announcer, as has on occasion been suggested. However, by January 1964 he had moved with his family to Australia's capital, Canberra. Eventually settling in Yarralumla, at 10 Tasman

Place, Lyons, Berneville-Claye managed to secure employment in the Training Branch of the Department of Territories – a government administrative department that existed between 1951 and 1968.

Having escaped the debt collectors in England, Berneville-Claye endeavoured to reinvent himself in the capital, but was unable to control his predilection for self-aggrandisement, exaggeration and flights of fancy. Just some three months after his arrival in the capital, *The Canberra Times* ran an article on him, on 25 April 1964 (Anzac Day), with the title 'Ex-Spy Prepares To Be Prepared'. The article ostensibly introduced Berneville-Claye as the new Senior Scout Leader of 2nd Canberra (Deakin) Boy Scouts, billing him as eminently suitable to the role of forming the Scouts into a first-rate Search and Rescue Unit. However, the article provided a wildly exaggerated and untruthful wartime profile, the information for which had clearly been provided by Berneville-Claye himself.

The newspaper's (Anzac Day) subtitle ran, 'One of the Top Five British Agents of World War II'. It went on to espouse that, 'In a career that reads like an Ian Fleming thriller, Mr Berneville-Claye worked behind enemy lines in the Western Desert with Colonel David Stirling's Special Air Service.' Thereafter he declared that he 'led Italian partisans in daring raids in Northern Italy and, under the codename *Le Corbeau* (chough), led a Maquis group in Auvergne in Central France'. Moreover, 'in 1944 he parachuted into Germany where he remained, working in a variety of disguises including that of an SS captain, until Berlin was overrun by the Russians in March 1945.' A little of this is loosely based on fact, but most of course is pure fantasy. It is interesting also to note that within this wartime synopsis Berneville-Claye chose to include, but adjust and change the spelling of, his derogatory nickname 'Chuff', to the more romantic moniker, 'chough' (a bird of the crow family).

His new Australian neighbours were encouraged to believe that this dashing military hero had first met his German-born wife, Gisela, when he had parachuted into Germany and used her father's Berlin home as a base for operations. Also, that he had been declared by the Head of SOE Germany, a certain 'Colonel Scotland', to be 'one of the top five British agents of World War II', as well as that he had been captured five times, been tortured by the Gestapo, but had nonetheless escaped from captivity on every occasion.

Furthermore, Berneville-Claye had let it be known that his family had supposedly believed him to be 'missing in action' for three years, and that upon his return to England at the end of the war, for all this derring-do he had won a Bar to his Military Cross. His first Military Cross had supposedly been awarded for commando work in the Western Desert, for his part in raids on Tobruk, Benghazi and Derna in September 1942. Additionally, for his daring work with the Maquis Resistance he had also supposedly received the Croix de Guerre from General de Gaulle.

Accompanying *The Canberra Times* article was a picture of Berneville-Claye at his Yarralumla home, surrounded by his young family, Andrew (age 12), Colin (age 11), Peter (age 9), Susan (age 6), and Lucky, the dog. As recalled later by Andrew, his eldest son, Berneville-Claye also continued to perpetuate the myth that he had been educated at Charterhouse and had an MA degree from Cambridge, as well as that he had retired from the SAS in the rank of major. Although his wife, Gisela, went along with this highly embellished and fabricated profile, she later acknowledged that it was all pure fantasy.

In contrast, home life for his young family was not as ideal as the picture Berneville-Claye painted for the press, for he liked to get his own way, and a domineering and controlling side to his personality often rose to the surface, along with an unpleasant temper. He did not like being challenged or contradicted, and consequently Andrew and Peter later both left the family home early.

Having thus made his debut in *The Canberra Times*, for a time thereafter Berneville-Claye regularly featured in its pages. It is also evident that he developed a predilection for writing to the newspaper's editor and, over the next three years, his letters were routinely published in the paper's 'Letters to the Editor' section. His interests appear to be diverse, and he commented upon a wide range of issues of the day, including economic, security, medical and, particularly, political. Regardless of whether one is inclined to agree or not with the thrust of his arguments, his letters generally reveal a degree of wit and eloquence.

Berneville-Claye's first such letter, under the title 'Sliding Costs', was published by the newspaper some two months after he had been introduced within its pages to Canberra Society as a supposed 'war hero'. It was a relatively light-hearted criticism concerning the fact that the Sydney Opera House was going to exceed its original cost estimate by some margin. Although amusing in tone, there is nonetheless a clear slight made against the professional capabilities of the ministers and public servants responsible for estimating such costs. In the coming years the tone of his criticism against public servants became more pointed and, even if a challenge might on occasion have been warranted, one detects that he harboured a general grievance against those in authority.

In August 1964, Berneville-Claye, by way of profession, established a 'finishing school' for young ladies. In promoting its launch, he was successful in securing self-publicity once again from *The Canberra Times*. The article on 12 August, under the title 'Cloak-and-Dagger Man in the Charm Business', summarised much of what had been published two months previously concerning Berneville-Claye's derring-do during the war. But this time it added that 'during this period he worked with the late Colonel [*sic*] Yeo-Thomas, better known as The White Rabbit'. In fact, Forest 'Tommy' Yeo-Thomas held the rank of wing commander in the RAF. He had died earlier that year, in February.

In terms of credentials for running a finishing school for fashion models, Berneville-Claye had evidently fed a certain line to the newspaper, this being that, after the war, he had been, as reported in the article, 'a theatrical producer, BBC television director and a film director with the Rank Organisation'. It was also stated that he had 'conducted drama courses for adult education authorities'. Although

Berneville-Claye evidently had a clear interest in drama and perhaps also scriptwriting, this of course amounts to a gross embellishment of his résumé in this regard.

When asked by the newspaper's reporter whether this initiative was somewhat unusual for an erstwhile 'cloak-and-dagger' man, Berneville-Claye is quoted as having said that 'although this might appear to be so on the surface, there was plenty of precedent. Yeo-Thomas, regarded by many as the master spy of World War II, had been a fashion designer from the house of Dior [*sic*].' This statement has reasonable basis, for before the war it seems that Yeo-Thomas worked in Paris for the fashion designer Edward Molyneux, who to some extent influenced Christian Dior in ladies' skirt fashion.

Berneville-Claye's 'finishing school' was duly established and later in that month of August advertisements were run in the same newspaper for the 'Models and Mannequins Course'. The commercial ran:

> Do you want the very best out of womanhood? Are you planning a career as a mannequin? Do you know the value of a 'Finishing School'? The Models and Mannequins course will give you elegance, Poise and Self-confidence. For an obligation-free discussion, telephone Douglas Berneville-Claye 77274.

Initially his 'finishing school' shared the premises of the Canberra Ballet School in Civic, the city centre of Canberra. However, he was hopeful of establishing his own studio in due course.

Berneville-Claye does not appear in the pages of *The Canberra Times* again that year for some four months, no doubt hard at work with his new business venture. But then, in December 1964, he penned the second of his letters to the editor, under the title 'Trade Union Tyranny'. He commenced by commenting, 'What scandalous tyranny is imposed by the trade union movement by forbidding men to work for extra money during their recreation leave. The effrontery of these officials is, apparently, boundless.' He goes on to argue that the unions had been established to protect working men from unscrupulous employers and that, given the difficult financial climate, the unions should not now exert their powers over those that they serve to deprive them from engaging in additional work. He concludes, 'There never was a greater need for a man to own the right to work as much as he wanted and needed to than right now. The last people in the world to prevent or deny them this right should be the unions.'

The following month, in January 1965, there were two further letters in quick succession to the editor. In the first, 'Immediate Inquest Desirable', Berneville-Claye expresses 'grave disquiet' over the accidental shooting by police of a criminal and calls for an inquest, 'before the case is stifled in departmental white-washing and political expediency'. The second letter, 'Ponderous Procedure of Naturalisation', bemoans the fact that he considers the application procedures for Australian citizenship, for which he was applying at the time, to be overly bureaucratic. He complains that he, as 'head of the family', is not allowed to apply on behalf of his family members, and that all are required to apply individually. With regard to the Australian Citizenship Convention, at the time in progress, he opined, 'I suppose it is to be expected that the deliberations will range from the serious and constructive to the plain ridiculous.'

Six months later, in July 1965, Berneville-Claye once again features in the 'Letters to the Editor' section. Under the title, 'Voting System Farcical', he berates the preferential voting system. He writes:

> it seems quite ridiculous to expect me to fill the ballot paper like a breakfast-cereal competition. ... To find a candidate defeated on the primary vote but elected on second preferences seems to me to be farcical and this must be frustrating to the electors, however satisfying to politicians. No wonder voting is compulsory. If it weren't, wild horses wouldn't drag me to the polls.

In this letter, we get a foretaste of things to come, as his missives become increasingly politically focused.

Meanwhile, a year on from its launch, Berneville-Claye's business foray into the fashion world was expanding in scope and appeared to be going well. A series of adverts were run in his newspaper of choice, over July 1965, promoting the 'Slenderette Health and Beauty Studios'. Three courses were offered: the 'Models and Mannequins Course (full professional training, or a complete finishing course); the Housewives Course (deportment, figure control, make-up, hair-care and styling, speech and etiquette); and the Junior Miss Course (finishing course for young ladies 12–16 years)'.

All these courses were billed as being under the personal tuition and supervision of Berneville-Claye, the company's general manager. His credentials were cited as a 'BBC TV director, film director with the Rank Organisation and years of experience in grooming the Rank Starlets'. His studio premises were at Garema Place, Civic, Canberra. Notwithstanding his false credentials, one may reasonably assume that Berneville-Claye made a good fist of his new profession, given his undoubted charm, supreme self-confidence, talent, and chameleon-like ability to adopt different personas.

A couple of further letters then arrived on the desk of the editor of *The Canberra Times* in quick succession. The first, that same month of July, 'Economic Jungle', and the second in August, 'Measles Vaccine', illustrate the somewhat eclectic nature of Berneville-Claye's interests. Thereafter, his letters focus increasingly on political issues of the day.

In late 1966, Berneville-Claye launched forth in a flurry of letters to the editor, only this time he appears to have reinvented himself as a political activist. Attacking the government of the day over its military conscription policies towards the Vietnam War, Berneville-Claye did not, however, limit his activities to writing letters to the newspaper. Associating himself with public anti-war demonstrations, he became increasingly irksome to the police, with unforeseen and fateful consequences for him.[2]

In view of the Vietnam War, conscription in Australia, or mandatory military service known as national service, had been reintroduced in 1964 under the Liberal leader, Prime Minister Robert Menzies. Under the National Service Act 1964, 20-year-old men were selected under a sortition or lottery draw, and obliged to provide two years' full-time service, followed by three years on the active reserve list. Moreover, the Defence Act was amended in May 1964 so that national servicemen could serve overseas, this being the first time since the Second World War. Then, in March 1966, the new Liberal leader, Prime Minister Harold Holt, announced that national servicemen would be sent to Vietnam to fight with Australian Regular Army units and with American forces. In the late 1960s, domestic opposition grew to both the Vietnam War and to Australian conscription.

Berneville-Claye's objection to such policies was first published in a letter, 'Liberals and Conscription', on 9 November 1966. Declaring himself to have been a supporter of Liberal or similar policies for some thirty years, he asserted that this was now impossible. He wrote:

> Does the retiring Liberal Government really believe that the hatred of their Vietnam and conscription policies is only a noisy and unimportant pocket? If this is the case, they have sacrificed their right to govern on behalf of the people. Or is it that they do not care; that they are, indeed, an oligarchy, believing themselves secure despite the electorate?

Against the backdrop of a federal election later that same month, Berneville-Claye asserted: 'The ALP [Australian Labor Party] did not foster the new movement; it was born out of the anxiety of a people too long ill-governed.' He went on to state that *The Canberra Times* had been providing one-sided prominence to the Liberal Party and to the views of Mr McMahon, a prominent Liberal minister who had overseen the National Service Act, and thus the reintroduction of conscription two years previously. Later that month, Berneville-Claye wrote again to the same newspaper. In his letter 'Government Should Go', he made a further direct attack upon the Liberal Party.

Berneville-Claye was no doubt aware that the manner of his introduction to Canberra society two years previously, in the same national newspaper, provided his views a certain prominence, particularly since his supposed eminence as a decorated war hero made his revelation as an anti-war campaigner even more dramatic. One assumes he held his view sincerely enough, but no doubt he also relished the opportunity to become once again the centre of attention. In an increasingly turbulent political period, with growing disaffection over Vietnam policies, and with the federal elections looming, here was an opportunity for him to be a part of great theatre.

However, Berneville-Claye's next move was one that set him on a course of being perceived as an ever-increasing thorn in the side of the police. In late November, a couple of days before polling day, he submitted a formal complaint to the police. This concerned Liberal Party election posters that had been placed along Commonwealth Avenue, between City Hill and Capital Hill. Berneville-Claye asserted that affixing such posters breached the Roads and Public Places Ordinance, which prohibited the billing of posters in public places.

To make clear his assertion, Berneville-Claye chose to publicly tear down a Liberal poster in front of the British High Commission. He was photographed doing so. The following day he appeared in *The Canberra Times*, in an article titled 'The ACT [Australian Capital Territory] Campaign: Police Action on Election Posters in City Area'. He had now placed himself on the police radar as a political agitator.

Following Holt's re-election victory, Berneville-Claye felt compelled to burst into print once more. In a letter, 'Demonstration of Contempt', published on 14 December 1966, he made clear his dissatisfaction with the Liberal Party's nominees for Parliament's Advisory Council. He wrote, 'Sir, flushed with its recent success, the Liberal oligarchy has made the first demonstration of contempt for democratic processes. ... We can expect more of this, and we shall have only ourselves to blame. ... Instances of this type of Government action will, no doubt, occur with infuriating frequency.' With an eye to the next elections in 1969, he then urged voters to dispense with the Liberal Party, writing: 'What in fact we ought to do is to demonstrate contempt for this sort of thing, and (a) reject this kind of Advisory Council out of hand, and (b) hurl this oligarchy out in 1969.'

The state visit to Australia by US President Lyndon Johnson a few months previously, in October 1966, had led to its fair share of anti-Vietnam War protestors making themselves heard, besides supporters of the cause. The visit to Australia of South Vietnam Prime Minister Nguyen Cao Ky, scheduled for January 1967, was anticipated to once again enliven the increasing trend of anti-war protests.

Berneville-Claye felt compelled to write again to the same national newspaper. In his letter 'No Decline in Hospitality', he makes clear his disdain for the Liberal Party. He declares:

> The present situation over Air Vice-Marshal Ky is not helped by abusing all who find his visit to Australia repugnant. ... When the visit was first mooted the Prime Minister heard sufficient to enable him to assess the wisdom of his action. ... That he chose to proceed in spite of public abhorrence was typical of the Liberals' lack of sensitivity to the feelings of the electorate. ... Surely then, as people of a free nation with established moral values, there exists an inalienable right to object to entertaining him.

This last letter to the editor was published the morning that Ky was scheduled to attend a press conference at the Hotel Canberra, on 18 January 1967. Some 200 anti-Vietnam War protestors, including Berneville-Claye, were there to meet him, gathered around a Vietcong flag, shouting at him and waving banners. The ACT police were reinforced by New South Wales police. There were scuffles with the NSW police, who then moved inside the barricades and arrested four of the demonstrators, who were charged with offensive behaviour and resisting arrest.

The press was also present at the demonstration, and Berneville-Claye took the opportunity to once again make his opinion known.

There was extensive coverage in the papers the following day. Under the article headline 'NSW Police Accused of Brutality', *The Canberra Times* ran the story:

> One witness, Mr D. Berneville-Claye, of Lyons, said he had seen police attack a man who was crouching in a corner, punching, and kicking him and finally hitting him with truncheons. The incident, Mr Berneville-Claye said, was a piece of unparalleled brutality. He attended the demonstration as a disinterested observer, he said, but was sickened by the police brutality. Mr Berneville-Claye called for a public enquiry into the clash.

Hitherto, Berneville-Claye's letters to the press, although forthright, had been acceptable in the cut and thrust of political debate within a liberal democracy. *The Canberra Times* had certainly perceived them as fit for publication, and no doubt appreciated that they offered an eloquent enough counterweight to the government's Vietnam War policies. Moreover, his earlier complaints to the police concerning the billing of Liberal posters, and associated antics in front of the British High Commission, may have irritated the police, but that had been all. However, by very publicly accusing the police of brutality and calling for a public enquiry, he had radically just changed the tempo.

The police had certainly acted firmly and, as some argued, possibly provocatively, in that they crossed the barricades to remove the Vietcong flag from the protestors. There had also been scuffles in which a few bruises had been sustained as police made their arrests, but nothing amounting to the serious allegations voiced by Berneville-Claye, as quoted in a national newspaper, which the police viewed as a gross exaggeration.

Berneville-Claye had now seriously upset the police and, in an article that appeared the following day, the ACT Commissioner of Police, Roy Wilson, robustly defended the action of both the ACT and NSW police forces. He also pointedly asked *The Canberra Times* whether the newspaper had asked Berneville-Claye to follow up his allegations in a signed statutory declaration.

Notwithstanding this, if Berneville-Claye had left matters there, then perhaps things might have simmered down. But he did not. Emboldened by and enjoying his limelight in the media, a few weeks later, on 6 March, he wrote further on the matter to ACT Commissioner of Police Roy Wilson. But he made the fateful error of signing his letter 'D.W. Berneville-Claye, MC, C de G, Major (ret'd)'.[3]

In the interim, Wilson had been doing his homework and, in doing so, had contacted the UK police at New Scotland Yard. Upon receiving and perusing the UK police correspondence, Wilson knew he had documentary evidence of Berneville-Claye's predilection to distort facts and convey lies. As such, his allegations of police brutality would be viewed as unreliable. However, Wilson did not leave it there. Within the week, Berneville-Claye was compelled to appear before the Canberra Court of Petty Sessions, on 10 March, charged with falsely representing himself as entitled to wear the Military Cross and the Croix de Guerre.

The court proceedings were extensively reported the following day, 11 March, under the title 'Man Fined For Claim to War Medals', on the front page of *The Canberra Times*, in time for all to read at leisure over that weekend. Following receipt of Berneville-Claye's letter, Commissioner Wilson had sent Detective Inspector Harold Luton and Detective Sergeant Charles Kent to Berneville-Claye's house in Tasman Place, Lyons.

When interviewed, Berneville-Claye had told the two detectives that he had been decorated in the Second World War for his action in the Western Desert and with Resistance forces in France and Italy. He first attempted to bluff that the medals were with his mother in England. But upon further questioning, he admitted that he had not received any awards other than normal campaign service ribbons. He also told the detectives that his supposed war record had started as a foolish act of vanity aboard the ship coming to Australia, and that it had subsequently been reported in a Melbourne newspaper, and thereafter he had never denied it.

However, this was not all that was reported. Detective Sergeant Kent also gave evidence regarding Berneville-Claye's record that had been received from New Scotland Yard. The newspaper also therefore reported that Berneville-Claye 'had been court-martialled three times and was cashiered from the Army in 1946'. Moreover, that he 'had convictions for unlawfully wearing military emblems, falsely representing himself to be a member of HM Forces, seven charges involving forged cheques, bigamy, stealing and fraudulent conversion'.

Throughout the court proceedings, Berneville-Claye, who was described as a company representative, age 49, and as being dressed in a dark suit, said very little. Nor was he represented. When asked by the magistrate, Clarence Hermes, whether he wished to make any comment, Berneville-Claye responded, 'I've nothing to say.' He pleaded guilty and was fined fifty Australian dollars. This was equivalent to a week's salary at the time, but this was not the main concern. Rather, Berneville-Claye knew that the deeply embarrassing court revelations meant that his time in Australia's capital was over.

What reputation Berneville-Claye had managed to build for himself, albeit underpinned by falsehoods, now lay in tatters. His flirtation with politics as an unlikely anti-war protestor and his ill-judged and vainglorious decision to cross swords with the police had led to his undoing. The fallout was rapid. At the beginning of the following week, *The Canberra Times* reported that, following his resignation, Berneville-Claye had been replaced as Convenor of the Lyons Festival Committee.

However, Berneville-Claye, besides being resilient, was of course by now a past master at reinventing himself, and it appears that he did not let this unduly set him back. He moved with his family to Campbelltown, some 33 miles south-west of Sydney, in New South Wales. Here, he managed to secure a teaching appointment in the English faculty of the prestigious Catholic boys' school, St Gregory's

College, located in the suburb of Gregory Hills. False claims to a Charterhouse School education and Oxbridge degrees no doubt helped him secure his appointment. Nonetheless, despite not having any teaching qualifications, given his inherent talent he became a well-respected teacher of English at the college.

Perhaps, having reached the age of 50, Berneville-Claye had finally learned from past mistakes, for, besides being an English teacher at St Gregory's College, he also became something of a pillar of the community. He was the secretary of Campbelltown Show Society, a committee member of Fisher's Ghost Festival, and a pioneer of Harlequin's Rugby Union Club. Furthermore, he was a candidate in the 1971 Council Election, during which he portrayed himself, in his election advertisements, as a man of 'vision, intellectual depth and experience'. Moreover, having converted to Roman Catholicism (an influence of the college, no doubt), he became calmer and more at peace with himself.[4]

Berneville-Claye did not confine himself entirely to Australia in his later years. He made a family visit to the UK, in 1974, and from this trip there survives a photograph of him in Trafalgar Square, London, feeding the pigeons.

Then, on 26 June 1975, seemingly unexpectedly and following just a short, two-week illness and aged just 57, Berneville-Claye died.[5] He was in the Randwick Chest Hospital, Sydney, which specialised in tuberculosis treatment, when he passed away. A few days later, on 30 June, a full and moving requiem mass was held for him in St Gregory's College Chapel, before his interment at St John's Catholic Cemetery, Campbelltown.[6]

His post-mortem subsequently revealed that he died of bronchopneumonia, and that underlying this was secondary lung cancer, which had progressed from initial prostate cancer. The cancer appears to have been diagnosed only post-mortem. Thus, mercifully for Berneville-Claye, he appears to have been unaware of it and not to have suffered overly.[7]

Following Berneville-Claye's death, glowing and emotional accolades were offered. He was eulogised as a man held in 'high esteem and respect', and locals paid tribute to him, focusing upon his public speaking skills, humour, and dedication to good causes. The mayor, Bob Barton, called him 'a gifted man with education and experience'. He was certainly an effective English teacher at St Gregory's College. Following his death there was a prize in his name – the 'Douglas Berneville-Claye Memorial Trophy' – for debating and public speaking, which was to be presented annually at the Year 12 Graduation Ceremony.[8]

Berneville-Claye's obituary states that he was a devoted family man, an inspired teacher of English at a Catholic boys' school, and a tireless worker for charity, including the Lions. It also mentions that he was involved in local politics and associated good causes, and that he was devoted to the Christian education of youth.

Had the leopard changed his spots? In some respects, it might seem to be the case, although not where forethought and consideration for his wife, Gisela, was concerned. Having converted to Roman Catholicism, Berneville-Claye was honoured with a full requiem mass. However, afterwards it transpired that he had let lapse his membership of the Returned Servicemen's League, and thus he was no longer insured for funeral expenses. In any event, he left Gisela penniless. On top of that, she was sued for debt and forced to pay back the 4,000 Australian dollars for funeral costs, which she did at a rate of five dollars a week. Consequently, Gisela was unable even to afford a headstone for his grave.[9]

It was many years before the citizens of Campbelltown came to realise that they had seen only one facet of Berneville-Claye. These days it may be difficult for some to comprehend how he had been able to move from location to location and reinvent himself, using the same untruths, without his past rapidly catching up with him.

It was only in 1989 that English engineer and computer scientist Sir Timothy Berners-Lee invented the World Wide Web, and the first web browser the following year, heralding the Internet and the 'Information Age'. Prior to this, information passage and distribution was, by comparison, incredibly limited and parochial. This had implications for all manner of records, including those of the police. Thus, there existed no Internet online search engines. Nor could one simply 'download' media articles or digital books, written and published around the world, at a touch of a button.

Even so, it was not until 2008 that Campbelltown citizens became aware of the extent of Berneville-Claye's past. The *Campbelltown Macarthur Advertiser* ran an article the following year, on 25 March, under the title 'Campbelltown Hero Linked to Nazis'. It led with the line, 'St Gregory's College has dumped the name of its traditional public speaking cup – the Douglas Berneville-Claye Trophy – after discovering that its namesake was a traitor.' Mr Tony Fitzgerald was a pupil at St Gregory's College at the time of Berneville-Claye's funeral in 1975, and later the deputy headmaster. He recalls that upon hearing revelations about him, the college felt compelled to remove his name from the senior debating and public speaking trophy.

Another St Gregory's College pupil, James Dampier, later recalled Berneville-Claye in his *Aussie History Podcast*, in April 2020. He recollected:

> He was my English teacher for two years. We all thought he was a war hero. He told us he had a bad back because the Nazis had tortured him, and that he was a spy who'd parachuted into Nazi Germany. When he died in 1975 from cancer, his funeral service was held in the school chapel. He was a pretty effective English teacher, even if he did like to talk too much about himself, almost all of it lies. I'm amazed that he got away with it for so long.

Other Campbelltown citizens had equal trouble reconciling what they had known of Berneville-Claye, as the revered English teacher, and what they were now discovering. Geoff Hicks, who had authorised Berneville-Claye's 1971 election material, said, 'This is very disappointing. It's an incredible story; stranger than fiction.

I feel particularly sorry for his family. I knew his wife and children really well and they were decent people.'[10]

Berneville-Claye left in his wake four wives and at least ten children that are known of, including Metcalfe, and two others that were put up for adoption. Some family members, including a few who had earlier received her warmly, began to question and resent Metcalfe's revelations in her book. She started to receive some vitriolic mail, plus a demand that she should get DNA testing done. This she said that she was content to do, so long as other family members shared the cost. Metcalfe said of some family members that 'They prefer to remember him as being handsome, charming and making a success of the last few years of his life, a respected father and grandfather.'

However, Berneville-Claye and the more colourful aspects of his character had long been in the public domain. Although Seth's book, published 1972, makes use of pseudonyms, it is not difficult to identify, in Chapter 15, the real 'Archibald Webster'. Weale, a military historian and an expert on the BFC, published a revised version of his book in 2002 (first published 1994), in which all names used are real, and in which he describes Berneville-Claye's record as 'an extraordinary farrago of dishonesty'.

Metcalfe's book, published 2002, provided her father a certain revised prominence. That same year, Mark Handscomb, a television and radio producer, created a thirty-minute radio documentary for BBC Radio 4, *It's My Story: In the Past Darkly*. During the making of the documentary, sons, daughters and daughters-in-law of Berneville-Claye were interviewed, and the programme was broadcast in April 2002.

Berneville-Claye's MI5 files, in the National Archives, are now a matter of open public record. Moreover, these days the World Wide Web and Internet also, of course, has a prominent part to play, and he is honoured with his own Wikipedia entry.

Douglas Berneville-Claye leaves a complex historical legacy, as a character of enormous international interest – charismatic and extremely talented, albeit flawed, and seemingly never overly concerned with learning from life's mistakes. One can't help but conclude that given his talents, his was a life of opportunity largely wasted, and regret the loss of what otherwise he might have achieved if he had applied himself positively. Regardless, he remains enigmatic and somewhat elusive.

Endnotes

Chapter 1: Early Life and Military Training

1. Church of England, Record of Births and Baptisms, London, 1813 to 1917.
2. Metcalfe, Margaret. *All My Father's Children* (Metcalfe, 2002), Ch. 5.
3. PRO, MI5 File KV2/626(1), Folio No. 24a (Personal Particulars) & 31a (Special Branch report).
4. *Sandhurst Cadet Entries*. Royal Military Academy, Sandhurst. His MI5 file (Army Particulars) records erroneously that he entered Sandhurst on 23.08.1941, albeit his commissioning date of 27.09.1941 is accurate. His Wikipedia entry suggests he preceded his Sandhurst training at Pwllheli, Wales.
5. *London Gazette* (Supplement 35303, Page 5851), 10 October 1941.
6. PRO, WO 166/4732, war diary 11th Battalion, West Yorkshire Regiment, Oct 1940–Dec 1941.
7. PRO, WO 166/9003, war diary 11th Battalion, West Yorkshire Regiment, Jan–May 1942.
8. PRO, WO 176/67, war diary 11th Battalion, West Yorkshire Regiment, Jun 1942–Jan 1944.
9. PRO, MI5 File KV2/626(2), Folio No. 11a, Copy of Minute, W.O. File No. P/207721, dated 12 May 1942.
10. PRO, WO 166/9002, war diary 2/5th Battalion, West Yorkshire Regiment, Jan–June 1942.

Chapter 2: L Detachment SAS – Operation BIGAMY

1. CAB 44/152, Commandos and Special Service Troops in the Middle East & North Africa. Sect. 7.

2. James [Pleydell], Malcolm. *Born of the Desert* (Collins, 1945), Ch. 13.

3. Almonds Windmill, Lorna. *Gentleman Jim* (Constable & Robinson, 2002), Ch. 10.

4. Mather, Carol. *When the Grass Stops Growing* (Pen & Sword, 1997), Ch. 18.

5. Gordon-Creed, Geoffrey & Field, Roger. *Rogue Male* (Coronet, 2011), Ch. 6.

6. Kennedy Shaw, W.B. *Long Range Desert Group* (Collins, 1945), Ch. 12.

7. James [Pleydell], Malcolm. *Born of the Desert* (Collins, 1945). Pleydell gave pseudonyms in his narrative to every man killed or wounded. However, the 2001 publication includes 'Notes to New Edition', in which David List, SAS Historian, provides the real names of these men. Nonetheless, it still remains unclear whether the driver to Richard Ardley was James Webster, or possibly Driver William Marlow RASC, both of whom died as a result of the raid.

8. Maclean, Fitzroy. *Eastern Approaches* (Jonathan Cape, 1949), Part 2, Ch. 5.

9. James [Pleydell], Malcolm. *Born of the Desert* (Collins, 1945), Chs. 17 & 18. Although the author incorrectly recalls in his narrative that it was Johnson who stayed behind, it was in fact Ritchie who did so.

Chapter 3: 1st SAS Regiment – Operations LIGHTFOOT & PALMYRA

1. PRO, MI5 File KV2/626(2), Folio No. 11a, Extract from Army Service Record, Berneville-Claye.

2. Ibid.

3. James [Pleydell], Malcolm. *Born of the Desert* (Collins, 1945), Ch 20.

4. Cowles, Virginia. *The Phantom Major* (Collins, 1958), Appendix.

5. SAS Regimental Association. *The SAS War Diary 1941–1945* (Extraordinary Editions, 2011).

6. James [Pleydell], Malcolm. *Born of the Desert* (Collins, 1945). 'Notes to New Edition' 2001, by David List (SAS Historian), and Appendix – 'Roll of Honour', compiled by David Buxton.

7. In her book, *All My Father's Children*, Margaret Metcalfe quotes the then secretary of the SAS Regimental Association as suggesting that Berneville-Claye served in B Squadron.
8. Davis, Peter. *SAS: Men in the Making* (Pen & Sword, 2015), Ch. 1.
9. WO 218/97, 1 SAS War Diary, Jan–Apr 1943.
10. PRO, MI5 File KV2/627(2), Folio No. 56B.

Chapter 4: Prisoner of War

1. PRO, MI5 File KV2/627(2), Folio No. 56b.
2. PRO, MI5 File KV2/626(1), Folio No. 22c.
3. Sonderführer were civilian specialists, given temporary military rank-range status, dependent upon specialism. Specialist Interpreters were generally given the equivalent rank of Oberfeldwebel (Warrant Officer Class II) in the Heer (Army).
4. PRO, MI5 File KV2/378, Captain E. Milton, Report 1, Para. 37 and 38.
5. Ibid., Para. 57 & 61.
6. Ibid., Para. 65.
7. PRO, MI5 File KV2/378, Captain E. Milton, Report 1, Para. 69–71 & Appx. II.
8. Ibid., Para. 70.
9. PRO, MI5 File KV2/626(2), Folio No. 3a.
10. Ibid., Folio No. 7a.
11. PRO, MI5 File KV2/627(1), Folio No. 106a.
12. PRO, MI5 File KV2/626(2), Folio No. 7a.
13. Ibid., Folio No. 8a.
14. Ibid., Folio No. 3a.

Chapter 5: Waffen-SS and British Free Corps

1. Weale, Adrian. *Renegades, Hitler's Englishmen*, Ch. 5. Cooper's MI5 file does not specify the 'grade' of badge, although Wikipedia suggests it was a 'Wound Badge in Silver'.

2. PRO, MI5 File KV2/254, Thomas Heller Cooper.

3. PRO, MI5 File KV2/626(2), Folio No. 14b.

Chapter 6: The English Officer

1. PRO, MI5 File KV2/626(2), Folio No. 14b.

2. PRO, MI5 File KV2/626(1), Folio No. 34b.

3. Ibid., Folio No. 27b.

4. PRO, MI5 File, KV2/254(3), Folio No. 47g.

5. PRO, MI5 File KV2/626(2), Folio No. 14b.

6. PRO, MI5 File KV2/439, Folio No. 6a.

7. PRO, MI5 File KV2/378, Captain E. Milton, Report 1, Para. 123.

8. PRO, MI5 File KV2/626(1), Folio No. 32a.

9. Ibid., Folio No. 53b.

10. Ibid., Folio No. 53a.

11. PRO, MI5 File KV2/627(2), Folio No. 70a.

12. PRO, MI5 File KV2/626(1), Folio No. 32b.

13. Ibid., Folio No. 34b.

Chapter 7: British Security Service (MI5) Investigation

1. PRO, MI5 File KV2/626(1), Folio No. 28a.

2. PRO, MI5 File KV 2/2828, Folio No. 102c. British Free Corps –
   Report dated 27/03/45.

3. PRO, MI5 File KV2/626(2), Folio No. 22a & 22b.

4. PRO, MI5 File KV2/626(1), Folio No. 22c.

5. Ibid., Folio No. 30a.

6. Ibid., Folio No. 39 & 41a.

7. Ibid., Folio No. 37.

8. Ibid., Folio No. 47b.

9. PRO, MI5 File KV2/627(2), Folio No. 58a.

10. Ibid., Folio No. 60a.

11. Ibid., Folio No. 69a & 73a.

12. PRO, MI5 File KV2/627(1), Folio No. 88b.

13. *News of the World*, report on Berneville-Claye court martial, 7 April 1946.
14. Metcalfe, Margaret. *All My Father's Children*, Ch. 23.
15. *News of the World*, report on Berneville-Claye bigamy trial, 30 June 1946.
16. PRO, MI5 File KV2/627(1), Folio No. 100a.
17. Ibid., Folio No. 109a.
18. PRO, MI5 File KV2/77, Theodore Schurch.

Chapter 8: Civvy Street

1. Williams, John. *Hume: Portrait of a Double Murderer* (Panther, 1958), Ch. 14.
2. Butler, Ivan. *Trials of Brian Donald Hume* (David & Charles, 1976), p. 81.
3. *The Times*, 'Trial of Brian Donald Hume', 26 January 1950.
4. Australian Broadcasting Corporation (ABC) Weekly, 15 July 1959, Vol. 21, No. 27, p. 12.
5. Metcalfe, Margaret. *All My Father's Children*, Photograph 15.
6. *The London Gazette (Supplement)*: 25 November 1958; 8 March 1963; 19 April 1963; 22 January 1965; 17 January 1974; 12 February 1974; 27 October 1981; & 3 December 1981.

Chapter 9: Australia

1. National Archives of Australia (NAA). Passenger Arrivals Index, 1898–1972.
2. Holt, Stephen. 'An Unlikely Leftist. Berneville-Claye' (*Honest History*, 7 October 2014).
3. Ibid.
4. *Campbelltown Macarthur Advertiser*, 25 March 2009.
5. *Sydney Morning Herald*, 28 June 1975, p. 112.
6. *Camden News*, 9 July 1975, p. 8.
7. Metcalfe, Margaret. *All My Father's Children* (Death Certificate), Ch. 12.

8. *Campbelltown Macarthur Advertiser*, 25 March 2009.

9. Metcalfe, Margaret. *All My Father's Children*, Ch. 14.

10. *Campbelltown Macarthur Advertiser*, 25 March 2009.

Glossary, Abbreviations and Acronyms

ACT	Australian Capital Territory
ALP	Australian Labor Party
ATS	Army Technical School
ATS	Auxiliary Territorial Service
AWOL	Absent Without Leave
BBC	British Broadcasting Corporation
BFC	British Free Corps
Camp PG	*Prigioniero di Guerra*: Prison of War Camp
C-in-C	Commander-in-Chief
CO	Commanding Officer (in command of a unit, e.g. a battalion)
DCLI	Duke of Cornwall's Light Infantry
DCO	Director/Directorate of Combined Operations
DCM	Distinguished Conduct Medal
DMO	Director/Directorate of Military Operations
DNA	Deoxyribonucleic acid [genetic testing]
DSO	Distinguished Service Order
Gestapo	Geheime Staatspolizei [Nazi Party's Secret State Police]
GOC	General Officer Commanding
GHQ	General Headquarters
G(RF)	General Staff (Raiding Forces)
Heer	German Army
ITC	Infantry Training Centre
JAG	Judge Advocate General
KGF	Kriegsgefangene [POW camps]
KGW	Kriegsgefangenenwesen [POW camps and affairs]
KOSB	King's Own Scottish Borderers

KSLI	King's Shropshire Light Infantry
LAF	Libyan Arab Force
LRDG	Long Range Desert Group
LVF	Légion des Volontaires Français
MA	Master of Arts [academic degree]
MBE	Member of the Most Excellent Order of the British Empire
MC	Military Cross
MI5	Military Intelligence, Section 5 [a.k.a. (British) Security Service]
MI6	Military Intelligence, Section 6 [a.k.a. Secret Intelligence Service]
MI9	Military Intelligence, Section 9
NCO	Non Commissioned Officer
NSW	New South Wales
OCTU	Officer Cadet Training Unit
Oflag	Offizierslager [German POW camp for officers]
POW	Prisoner of War
RA	Royal Artillery
RAC	Royal Armoured Corps
RAF	Royal Air Force
RASC	Royal Army Service Corps
RLC	Royal Logistic Corps
RSM	Regimental Sergeant Major
SAS	Special Air Service
SBO	Senior British Officer
SBS	Special Boat Section/Squadron/Service
SD	Sicherheitsdienst (SS Intelligence and Security Service)
SERE	Survival, Evasion, Resistance and Escape
SIB	Special Investigation Branch [of Military Police]
SIG	Special Interrogation Group
SIS	Secret Intelligence Service [a.k.a. MI6]
SNCO	Senior Non Commissioned Officer
SOE	Special Operations Executive

SO3	Staff Officer Grade 3
SS	Schutzstaffel [Nazi paramilitary organization]
SSR	Special Service Regiment
Stalag	Stammlager [German POW camp for 'other ranks']

Bibliography

Almonds Windmill, Lorna. *Gentleman Jim: The Wartime Story of a Founder of the SAS and Special Forces* (Constable & Robinson, 2002)

Asher, Michael. *The Regiment: The Real Story of the SAS: The First Fifty Years* (Viking, 2007)

Bender, Roger & Taylor, Hugh. *Uniforms, Organisation and History of the Waffen-SS* (Bender, 1969)

Berneville-Claye, Gloria. *The Lady Anne* (Amazon, 2018)

Berneville-Claye, Graeme. *Tied to the Mast* (Amazon, 2018)

Bradford, Roy & Dillon, Martin. *Rogue Warrior of the SAS: Lt Col 'Paddy' Blair Mayne* (John Murray, 1987)

Butler, Ivan. *Trials of Brian Donald Hume* (David & Charles, 1976)

Byrne, J.V. *The General Salutes a Soldier: With the SAS and Commandos in World War Two* (Hale, 1986)

Cooper, Artemis. *Cairo in the War 1939–1945* (Hamish Hamilton, 1989)

Cowles, Virginia. *The Phantom Major: The Story of David Stirling and the SAS Regiment* (Collins, 1958)

Davis, Peter. *SAS: Men in the Making* (Pen & Sword, 2015)

De Slade, Marquis. *The Yeoman of Valhalla: Behind the Siegfried Line* (private pub, 1970)

Gordon-Creed, Geoffrey & Field, Roger. *Rogue Male* (Coronet, 2011)

Hastings, Stephen. *The Drums of Memory: An Autobiography* (Pen & Sword, 1994)

Hoe, Alan. *David Stirling: The Authorised Biography of the Creator of the SAS* (Little Brown, 1992)

Ireland, Josh. *The Traitors: A True Story of Blood, Betrayal and Deceit* (Murray, 2017)

James [Pleydell], Malcolm. *Born of the Desert: With the SAS in North Africa* (Collins, 1945)

Jefferson, David. *Tobruk: A Raid Too Far* (Robert Hale, 2013)

Kelly, Saul. *The Hunt for Zerzura: The Lost Oasis and the Desert War* (Butler & Tanner, 2002)

Kemp, Anthony. *The SAS at War 1941–1945* (Penguin, 1991)

Kennedy Shaw, W.B. *Long Range Desert Group: The Story of its Work in Libya 1940–1943* (Collins 1945)

Ladd, James D. *SAS Operations: More than Daring* (Robert Hale, 1986)

Landwehr, Richard. *Britisches Freikorps: British Volunteers of the Waffen-SS 1943–45* (Merriam, 2008)

Littlejohn, David. *Foreign Legions of the Third Reich* (Bender, 1977)

Lloyd Owen, David. *Providence Their Guide: The Long Range Desert Group 1940–45* (Harrap, 1980)

Macintyre, Ben. *SAS Rogue Heroes: The Authorized Wartime History* (Viking, 2016)

Maclean, Fitzroy. *Eastern Approaches* (Jonathan Cape, 1949)

Marrinan, Patrick. *Colonel Paddy: The Man Who Dared* (Ulster Press, 1960)

Mather, Carol. *When the Grass Stops Growing: A War Memoire* (Pen & Sword, 1997)

Metcalfe, Margaret. *All My Father's Children: A Personal Journey* (Metcalfe, 2002)

Moorehead, Alan. *African Trilogy: The Desert War 1940–1943* (Hamish Hamilton, 1945)

Morgan, Mike. *Sting of the Scorpion: The Inside Story of the Long Range Desert Group* (Sutton, 2000)

Mortimer, Gavin. *Stirling's Men: The Inside History of the SAS in World War II* (Cassell, 2005)

Murphy, Sean. *Letting the Side Down: British Traitors of the Second World War* (History Press, 2005)

Oates, Jonathan. *Donald Hume: Notorious Bank Robber and Double Murderer* (Pen & Sword, 2020)

Pleasants, Eric. *I Killed to Live: The Story of Eric Pleasants, as Told to Eddie Chapman* (Cassell, 1957)

Pleasants, Eric (Sayer, Ian & Botting, Douglas, eds.). *Hitler's Bastard: Through Hell and Back in Nazi Germany and Stalin's Russia* (Mainstream, 2003)

Ross, Hamish. *Paddy Mayne: Lt Col Blair 'Paddy' Mayne, 1 SAS Regiment* (Sutton, 2003)

SAS Regimental Association. *The SAS War Diary 1941–1945* (Extraordinary Editions, 2011)

Scott, Michael. *Special Forces Commander: The Life and Wars of Peter Wand-Tetley OBE MC, Commando, SAS, SOE & Paratrooper* (Pen & Sword, 2011)

Seth, Ronald. *Jackals of the Reich: Hitler's British Korps* (New English Library, 1972)

Seth, Ronald. *A Spy has no Friends* (Headline, 2008)

Stein, George. *Waffen-SS: Hitler's Elite Guard at War* (Cornell UP, 1966)

Stevens, Gordon. *The Originals: The Secret History of the Birth of the SAS in their Own Words* (Ebury Press, 2005)

Strawson, John. *A History of the SAS Regiment* (Guild Ltd, 1985)

Sutherland, David. *He Who Dares: Recollections of Service in the SAS, SBS and MI5* (Leo Cooper, 1998)

Thesiger, Wilfred. *The Life of My Choice* (Collins, 1987)

Timpson, Alastair, with Gibson-Watt, Andrew. *In Rommel's Backyard: A Memoir of the Long Range Desert Group* (Leo Cooper, 2000)

Warner, Philip. *The Special Air Service* (Kimber & Co. Ltd, 1971)

Weale, Adrian. *Patriot Traitors: Roger Casement, John Amery and the Real Meaning of Treason* (Viking, 2001)

Weale, Adrian. *Renegades: Hitler's Englishmen* (Pimlico, 2002)

West, Rebecca. *The Meaning of Treason* (Macmillan, 1949)

Williams, John. *Hume: Portrait of a Double Murderer* (Panther, 1961)

Wynter, H.W. *Special Forces in the Desert War 1940–1943* (PRO War Histories, 2001)

Articles

Holt, Stephen. *'An Unlikely Leftist: Douglas Berneville-Claye'* (*Honest History*, 7 October 2014)

Wheatley, Ben. 'Revisited, The Security Services Investigation of British Abwehr/SD Agent Ronald Sydney Seth' (*Journal of Intelligence History*, Vol. 16, Issue 2, 2017)

Newspapers

The London Gazette (Supplement):

10 October 1941, Issue 35303, p. 5851, *Commissions*
7 January 1947, Issue 37843, p. 163, *Cashiered*
25 November 1958, Issue 41557, p. 7239, *Receiving orders*
25 November 1958, Issue 41577, p. 7240, *First meetings and public examinations*
25 November 1958, Issue 41577, p. 7242, *Adjudications*
8 March 1963, Issue 42838, p. 2175, *Intended Dividends*
19 April 1963, Issue 42972, p. 3456, *Dividends*
22 January 1965, Issue 43556, p. 875, *Release of Trustees*
17 January 1974, Issue 46184, p. 725, *Intended Dividends*
12 February 1974, Issue 46208, p. 1947, *Dividends*
27 October 1981, Issue 48777, p. 13658, *Intended Dividends*
3 December 1981, Issue 48812, p. 15443, *Dividends*

The Times:

26 January 1950, report on Trial of Brian Donald Hume

Sunday Pictorial:

16 June 1958, report on Confession of Brian Donald Hume

News of The World:

7 April 1946, 'Ex ATS Girl Says She Visited Billet' (report on court martial)
30 June 1946, 'Girl Prime Mover In My Wedding at 17' (report on bigamy trial)

The Canberra Times:

25 April 1964, p. 7, 'Ex-Spy Prepares To Be Prepared'

20 June 1964, p. 2, Letters to the Editor, 'Sliding Costs'

12 August 1964, p. 10, 'Cloak-and-Dagger Man in the Charm Business'

18 & 22 August 1964, p. 11, Advertisement, 'The Models and Mannequins Course'

18 December 1964, p. 2, Letters to the Editor, 'Trade Union Tyranny'

7 January 1965, p. 2, Letters to the Editor, 'Immediate Inquest Desirable'

23 January 1965, p. 2, Letters to the Editor, 'Ponderous Procedure of Naturalisation'

2 July 1965, p. 2, Letters to the Editor, 'Voting System Farcical'

8 & 10 & 12 July 1965, Advertisement, 'Slenderette Health and Beauty Studios'

21 July 1966, p. 2, Letters to the Editor, 'Economic Jungle'

30 August 1966, p. 2, Letters to the Editor, 'Measles Vaccine'

9 November 1966, p. 2, Letters to the Editor, 'Liberals and Conscription'

18 November 1966, p. 2, Letters to the Editor, 'Government Should Go'

25 November 1966, p. 13, 'The ACT Campaign: Police Action on Election Posters'

14 December 1966, p. 2, Letters to the Editor, 'Demonstration of Contempt'

18 January 1967, p. 2, Letters to the Editor, 'No Decline in Hospitality'

19 January 1967, pp. 1 & 11, 'NSW Police Accused of Brutality'

20 January 1967, p. 3, 'Methods of NSW Police Backed'

11 March 1967, p. 1, 'Man Fined for Claim to War Medals'

13 March 1967, p. 7, Announcement, 'New Convenor of Festival'

Sydney Morning Herald:

28 June 1975, p. 112, 'Obituary notice: Berneville-Claye'

Camden News:

9 July 1975, p. 8, 'Show Secretary Dies Suddenly'

The Scotsman:

8 September 2002, 'The Legion of Traitors'

Campbelltown Macarthur Advertiser:

25 March 2009, 'Campbelltown "Hero" Linked to Nazis'

National Archives, Kew, Surrey

Cabinet Office Papers:

CAB 44/151, history of Long Range Desert Group, Jun 1940 to Mar 1943

CAB 44/152, history of Commandos and Special Service Troops in the Middle East and North Africa, Jan 1941–Apr 1943

War Office Papers:

WO 201/721, history, L Detachment SAS Brigade and 1 SAS Regiment, 1941–1942

WO 201/732, special forces: operational questions, Mar 1942–Jan 1943

WO 201/735, reports of operations: raiding forces at Benghazi, Sep 1942

WO 201/743, GHQ operation instructions, raiding forces, Sep–Oct 1942

WO 201/747, battle file SAS, Oct–Nov 1942

WO 201/785, history L Detachment SAS Brigade, May–Jun 1942

WO 201/2257, raids on enemy lines of communications: Tobruk, Benghazi, Barce

WO 416/28/92, Berneville-Claye – German Record Cards of British POW

WO 416/408/98, Eric Pleasants – German Record Cards of British POW

WO 416/257/129, Alfred Vivian Minchin – German Record Cards of British POW

WO 416/28/227, Kenneth Edward Berry – German Record Cards of British POW

WO 416/239/88, Alexander MacKinnon – German Record Cards of British POW

WO 204/12796 & WO 204/13021, Theodore J.W. Schurch

WO 204/12856, British Renegades – G2 Intelligence, Arrest and Detention Reports

War Diaries:

WO 166/4732, war diary 11th Battalion, West Yorkshire Regiment, Oct 1940–Dec 1941

WO 166/9003, war diary 11th Battalion, West Yorkshire Regiment, Jan–May 1942

WO 176/67, war diary 11th Battalion, West Yorkshire Regiment, Jun 1942–Jan 1944

WO 166/9002, war diary 2/5th Battalion, West Yorkshire Regiment, Jan–June 1942

WO 218/96, war diary 1 SAS, Oct–Dec 1942

WO 218/97, war diary 1 SAS, Jan–Apr 1943

British Security Service (MI5) Files:

KV2/76–77, Theodore J.W. Schurch

KV2/254, Thomas Heller Cooper

KV2/245–250 & KV2/346, Margaret Joyce

KV2/377–380, Ronald Sydney Seth

KV2/439, John Boucicault de Suffield Calthrop

KV2/626–627, Douglas Webster St Aubyn Berneville-Claye

KV2/2828, British Free Corps

Special Operations Executive (SOE) Files:

HS9/1344–1345, Report of Operation BLUNDERHEAD / Ronald Seth

Home Office Files:

HO 45/25773, Amery, John: Renegades suspected or convicted of assisting the enemy

HO 45/25780 & 45/22405 & 45/22406, Joyce, William ('Lord Haw-Haw'): Renegades suspected or convicted of assisting the enemy

HO 45/25805, Cooper, Thomas: Renegades suspected or convicted of assisting the enemy

HO 45/25817, Minchin, Alfred Vivian: Renegades suspected or convicted of assisting the enemy

HO 45/25820, Berry, Kenneth Edward: Renegades suspected or convicted of assisting the enemy

Radio:

BBC Radio 4, *It's My Story: In the Past Darkly* (1 & 20 April 2002)

Film:

Channel 5 Broadcasting Ltd, *The Brits Who Fought for Hitler* (2002)

Index of People

Military ranks given are those generally highest achieved, as covered in the text, not necessarily those later achieved.